SO-BYP-655

ADVANCE PRAISE

FOR *TAKE THE LEAP*

BARBARA CORCORAN

"This book doesn't just tell you that you can change your life. It shows you how. *Take the Leap* is filled with valuable advice for any budding entrepreneur, along with the stories to back it up."

BOBBI BROWN

"I've always believed that a fresh perspective is the key to disrupting an industry or acing a new career. I've switched up my career multiple times and it keeps things interesting. If you are ready to go for the life and the job you really want, *Take the Leap* is the go-to book for anyone making a career change."

SIMON DOONAN

"Get ready to leap! A great career should be like a roller coaster: exhilarating, scary, with lots of sharp turns."

TAKE TH
LEA

CHANGE YOUR CAREER, CHANGE YOUR LIFE

SARA BLISS

G

GALLERY BOOKS

New York London Toronto Sydney New Delhi

G

Gallery Books
An Imprint of Simon & Schuster, Inc.
1230 Avenue of the Americas
New York, NY 10020

Copyright © 2018 by Sara Bliss

All rights reserved, including the right to reproduce this book or portions thereof
in any form whatsoever. For information, address Gallery Books Subsidiary
Rights Department, 1230 Avenue of the Americas, New York, NY 10020.

This Gallery Books trade paperback edition November 2023

GALLERY BOOKS and colophon are registered trademarks of
Simon & Schuster, Inc.

For information about special discounts for bulk purchases,
please contact Simon & Schuster Special Sales at 1-866-506-1949 or
business@simonandschuster.com.

The Simon & Schuster Speakers Bureau can bring authors to your
live event. For more information or to book an event, contact the
Simon & Schuster Speakers Bureau at 1-866-248-3049 or visit our
website at www.simonspeakers.com.

Interior design by Laura Palese

Manufactured in the United States of America

1   3   5   7   9   10   8   6   4   2

The Library of Congress has cataloged the hardcover edition as follows:

Names: Bliss, Sara, author.
Title: Take the leap: change your career, change your life / by Sara Bliss.
Description: New York: Touchstone, [2018]
Identifiers: LCCN 2018034914 | ISBN 9781501183188 (hardcover)
Subjects: LCSH: Career changes. | Vocational guidance.
Classification: LCC HF5384 .B55 2018 | DDC 650.14—dc23 LC record
available at https://lccn.loc.gov/2018034914

ISBN 978-1-6680-5273-0

FOR
ELLIOTT
& LIV

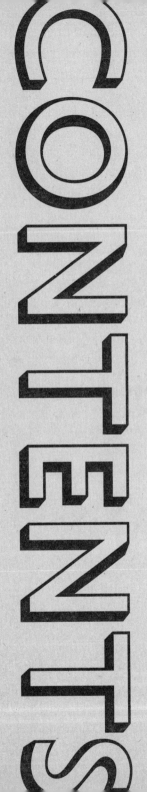

CONTENTS

UNLEASH YOUR CREATIVE SIDE

LAUNCH YOUR OWN BUSINESS

CHOOSE YOUR OWN ADVENTURE

GIVE BACK

FOLLOW YOUR BLISS

BECOME A WELLNESS WARRIOR

BECOME A PROFESSIONAL FOODIE

INTRODUCTION

—◆—

ADMIT IT. *You sometimes fantasize about living a completely different life.*

WHATEVER IT IS THAT you sometimes dream about, what if it could actually be your life? Maybe you want to turn your hobby into a career, be your own boss, launch your own business, or swap life in a cubicle for a job outdoors. Maybe you want to cash in on the tech boom or sell your screenplay. Or maybe you want to make your life about something bigger—you want to help people when they need it most, transform lives, and really make an impact.

Or perhaps you aren't looking to change anything at all, thank you very much, but everything around you is changing and you have no choice. Your company is being bought out. You got laid off. Your industry is shrinking or disappearing altogether. Your only option is to find an income-producing alternative, STAT. Whatever your reason for picking up this book, know that you absolutely can reinvent your life—and in these pages, you will meet sixty amazing people who will tell you exactly how.

Many of us grew up in an era when our parents chose one career and stuck to it for life. The world of work has radically changed since then. According to the Bureau of Labor Statistics, today only nine percent of Americans have the same employer for more than twenty years. While technology has shrunk entire industries (magazine publishing and stock trading are two examples), it has also made things possible that simply weren't imaginable fifteen years ago. Thanks to the internet, it has never been easier to apply for jobs, network, learn a new skill, take a class, market yourself, start a business, work remotely, or reinvent your career.

Yet we are still asking kids to pick what they want to do at eighteen. We are still promoting the idea that success means staying in one lane. How we perceive careers has to adapt to the possibilities that exist today. We have gotten comfortable with the idea of changing employers every few years. We need to be as comfortable with changing careers.

I wrote *Take the Leap* to share what I wish I knew when I was starting out—that who you are in one decade doesn't have to be who you are in the next. I came up with the concept for the book at a time when I was worried about my own career. I had already pivoted from the art world to magazines. I managed to build up a successful freelance writing business and wrote a couple of books, but then the financial crisis of 2008 hit and the magazine industry started shrinking rapidly. My editors were getting laid off, publications were folding, and my work was being devalued. Some of the top outlets started paying just $50 for an online article, or paying based on the number of views—certainly not enough to cover the bills. I knew I had to pivot fast.

As the number of available magazine opportunities shrank, I noticed that lifestyle brands were hiring former magazine staffers to work on online content, books, blogs, in-house magazines, marketing, and PR. The brands saw an opportunity to create their own messaging without having to rely on dwindling editorial coverage. I jumped into this new side hustle, happy to find a chance to write, consult, and get paid. It also allowed me to be selective about the editorial projects I took, focusing on profiles and travel.

While I was reinventing my own career, I noticed a trend happening with many of the people I was writing about. From celebrities to CEOs to founders to artists, I saw that the most successful people didn't always follow a linear path. Many went through multiple different careers with plenty of detours, so-called failures, and moments when they felt totally discouraged before they found what clicked. For anyone who hasn't found their groove, there is something so inspiring about people who found success a little later. I knew compiling those stories of transformation in a book would be very powerful for anyone wanting to pivot.

> "
> *When you are thinking of* **MAKING A MOVE,** *the best people to listen to are always* THE ONES WHO HAVE DONE IT.

I pitched the idea of *Take the Leap* as a book to an agent around 2009—but ended up on another career detour. As publishing began to look more toward high-profile people to sell books, it opened up a thriving market for ghostwriters, and I was directed there. The response to my pitch was that the idea was a magazine article, not a book, and that while I was a strong writer and had a couple of books under my belt, I wasn't successful or well-known enough to sell another one on my own. It was discouraging to say the least.

I started ghostwriting books as another side hustle, thinking that I would write my own books *later*. But thanks to constant assignments and two kids, "later" became years. And after a decade writing more than seven books anonymously or as a co-author, several of which were bestsellers, I knew I had to get my idea out there *now*. I got referrals for new agents, took meetings, and finally found agent extraordinaire Alison Fargis, who agreed that *Take the Leap* needed to be out in the world. We sent it out to editors, there was a bidding war between publishers, and *Take the Leap* was born.

I spent the next year researching the most inspiring, diverse group of leapers, because when you are thinking of making a move, the best people to listen to are always the ones who have done it. People who have radically changed their lives provide serious inspiration for everyone who has ever wanted to switch gears but worried they were too old, too young, or too broke to go for that dream. They have faced all the obstacles you can imagine—disapproving friends, lack of cash, nagging doubts, and steep learning curves. Yet they dived in anyway, went back to school, found mentors, ignored naysayers, and sometimes took steps backward before leaping forward toward the life they really wanted.

It turns out that changing careers is less about changing the job and more about changing your life. Whether you want more sanity and less stress, to find a greater purpose, be in charge of your own destiny, make more money, or follow that dream you just can't let go of—you're in the right place.

Now let's get started.

SARA BLISS

FROM ▶ **TO**

AUCTION HOUSE FRONT DESK ASSISTANT

WRITER AND BRAND ADVISOR

IT ALL STARTE

1

UNLEASH
YOUR
CREATIVE
SIDE

Sell Your Screenplay / Write Comics /
Find Work That Makes You Happy /
Make Art for Everyone / Star in Your Own Show

YOU FOUND THAT THING THAT LIGHTS YOU UP. Whether you are onstage, creating characters, belting out songs, covering a canvas in color, hitting the high notes, banging that drum, or imagining totally new worlds, you found how you want to spend every spare second.

But it's just a hobby. It won't make money. You're too old to break in now. It's not a real job. Is that what you tell yourself? What you hear from your friends?

There's this idea that being an adult means shutting the creative side of you down (or letting it come out only on weekends). That growing up means focusing solely on job security and 401(k)s.

Is it a challenge to make money in the arts? Yes; I can attest to that. Is there a tremendous amount of time and pressure and hard work that comes with trying to perfect your craft? Yes; it can be downright exhausting. But it is so rewarding to create. Nothing else compares.

There are always going to be reasons not to pivot, especially toward the arts, where the pay can be low and competition is fierce. This chapter celebrates people who have figured out how to navigate the obstacles that can come with a creative path. They worked to perfect a craft that they were only okay at when they began. They figured out how to monetize their work and found side gigs to support their goal if needed. They overcame self-doubt or the idea that they didn't have what it takes to succeed. They figured out a way in.

You can, too.

SELL YOUR
SCREENPLAY

LAURYN KAHN

FROM  **TO**

REALITY TV PRODUCTION ASSISTANT ▸ ▸ **SCREENWRITER**

I **DIDN'T PLAN ON BECOMING** a writer. I studied TV and radio at Ithaca College. I took one personal-essay class my senior year and realized I loved it. I had that one teacher who said, "You have an original style. You should keep writing." I still never thought I would make it as a writer, though. It felt like a pipe dream.

After college, I worked in New York as a production assistant in reality TV on *The Bachelor* and *Elimidate*. Then I moved to LA and continued PA'ing. It was the bottom rung: long days making no money, doing everything from cleaning to lunches to wiping up kids' pee.

For fun, I started sending emails out to friends where I would write my bitter, funny, out-of-the-box thoughts on life. A friend finally wrote back and said, "Just admit you have a blog!" So I made one called *Kahnicles of Life* just to make my friends laugh and have an outlet.

Then, like everyone else in LA, I had that moment when I decided to write a screenplay. I had no idea what I was doing, though—I barely knew the format. I didn't have an outline. I just started writing. It felt like the most overwhelming, difficult, confusing thing anyone can do. I eventually gave up.

I didn't have any friends who were writing or in comedy until I met another reality TV PA who wanted to break into that world, too. Her name was Lauren Palmigiano, and it was this amazing moment when I finally met someone like me. She was interning at Upright Citizens Brigade. It opened up this whole new comedy world to me that I desperately wanted to be a part of.

In 2007, Lauren landed a job working with Adam McKay and Will Ferrell at their new production company, Gary Sanchez Productions. It truly felt like the coolest job ever, and I started stalking Lauren about job openings. Then a life-changing moment happened when Adam was getting ready to direct a movie called *Step Brothers* and needed an assistant. Lauren got me an interview and I actually landed the job.

The week I started, Adam and Will launched Funny or Die, a website for short-form comedy. It immediately blew up. They were willing to give everyone a shot to produce content for the site, so I started coming up with ideas. Adam taught me how to write sketches. He thought I was funny, and that gave me confidence. He turned out to be my biggest mentor.

I was working as Adam's assistant full-time but always made time to write. If you want something bad enough, you just do it. I wrote sketches for Funny or Die for a couple of years, but I never wrote anything longer because I didn't think I was good enough and it all seemed too scary. Adam told me to just try. His advice: "Write what you want to see, and you can't go wrong." It was the push I needed.

My first pilot was called *Haters*. It was like *Sex and the City* if they were all female Larry Davids from New Jersey living in LA. I wrote it like no one was going to read it: the formatting was wrong, there weren't three acts, it was ridiculous and filled with bad language. But it was what I would want to watch. Adam eventually read it and not only did he think it was good, he told me he thought I could sell it and he wanted to put his name on it as a producer. That's when everything got a little crazy.

Adam gave me some notes and mentioned it to his agents. WME (William Morris Endeavor) read it and really loved it. They brought me in and said, "We aren't bringing you in because you're Adam's assistant, we're bringing you in because we want to focus on you." That's what got me signed.

I ended up selling *Haters* to MTV. But it wasn't an MTV-type show. So even though they bought it, they didn't know what to do with it and like many things in Hollywood it never got made. That's when my agent told me to think of a movie.

I had the nugget of an idea based on my one friend who was really good at internet stalking. It was about dating in the internet age and being able to find out everything about someone before you meet them. This time I read a great screenplay book called *Save the Cat*. My eyes were opened. Of course I couldn't write a screenplay when I first started—there's a process!

I gave myself a timeline to finish the script on the side: outline from January to March, write from March to June. I wrote two to three pages a day.

When I finally finished I did a few rounds of notes with friends, my agents, and Gary Sanchez, who was producing it, and we decided it was ready. Once it was, we sent it out, and it started a bidding war. I was making an assistant salary at the time. My *Haters* pilot had sold for $18K, so after agent fees and taxes, I got $8K (which was more money than I'd ever seen). For this script, the price went up to $400,000. That night, as I was driving home, the producer called and made me come back to the office. When I got there he said: "You need to make a decision by eight p.m. Fox 2000 is offering you one million dollars."

My coworkers always play pranks, so I didn't believe it. I might have cursed them out and almost left, but they swore it was real. I went from an assistant's salary to closing a million-dollar deal in one day. It was the craziest, most unexpected thing to ever happen to me.

However, the reality of Hollywood is a lot of things don't get made. The movie was on the fast track, but it switched studios, had a bunch of different actresses attached, and we ended up pulling the plug on it five weeks out from production because of some unforeseen issues. It was really heartbreaking.

> 66
>
> *I went from an assistant's salary to closing a* **MILLION-DOLLAR DEAL** *in one day.*

In the meantime, I kept writing and thinking ahead, instead of focusing on what wasn't happening. I was selling everything I wrote, which was exciting, but I was ready to get something made. In 2013, I wrote another script that was even closer to my heart about me and my friends taking a crazy trip to Spain. It was like *The Hangover* for girls meets *Lost in Translation*. I wanted it to be an accessible, real story about female friendship and that feeling you get when you go on vacation out of the country and you can kind of be anyone you want.

I sold it to Sony initially, but after two years and lots of notes from different executives coming in and out, it became something I wasn't proud of anymore. At that point, Sony had become a different studio and just wasn't going to make it. Then a production company called Good Universe, who I'd worked with on my first film, said they wanted to go back to my original screenplay and make it with a different studio. Sony let it go, and Netflix bought it and wanted to make it exactly how we wanted. Gillian Jacobs, Vanessa Bayer, and Phoebe Robinson play the three friends, and Richard Madden is the love interest. It is called *Ibiza* and premiered in May 2018, and you can watch it on Netflix right now!

I finally feel comfortable saying I'm a writer. Every year I get more confident and learn more. I really believe that if you have a voice or a story to tell, you can get there. I think the hardest part is starting. I have so many friends who have an idea in their head, but few actually write it and few take the time to work on it, get notes from people, and just hustle with it. It doesn't have to be perfect, you just have to do it.

BE AN
ARTIST
(WITHOUT THE STARVING PART)

LISA CONGDON

FROM

—

**FIRST-GRADE
TEACHER**

TO

—

**ILLUSTRATOR,
PAINTER, WRITER**

T**HERE IS SOMETHING INHERENTLY** joyful about Lisa Congdon's colorful artwork. Lisa left a career in education to become a full-time illustrator at age 40. The author of seven books, including *Art, Inc.: The Essential Guide for Building Your Career as an Artist,* Lisa has made a point of proving the starving-artist myth wrong.

What jobs did you have before you became an artist? Was there any connection between them?

I was a teacher for seven years before working at an education nonprofit where I managed projects and did a lot of writing and collaborating with colleagues. When I left that job to become an artist, it never occurred to me that I would be using those skills again. I had this idea that I was leaving behind this life to go sit at a drawing table and drink tea and listen to NPR. What I had to learn pretty quickly was that if you're going to be successful and make money, you have to be good at communicating with people, managing your schedule, and running a business.

Why did you decide to pursue illustration specifically?

I started with fine art but I quickly moved to illustration. As a fine artist, you have a lot more freedom in terms of what you create, but selling original art is really a hard way to make money. Also, quite frankly, illustration was the way that I could make a living. Through licensing my work, getting assignments, or illustrating books, I could get paid.

You were 40 when you began you career as an illustrator. What were the pros and cons of starting at that age?

In some ways I had a leg up because I had a lot of work and life experience, but I had a lot of competition in terms of who else was vying for the same illustration jobs. I had to really find a way to stand out. I did have self-doubt, but because I already had eighteen years of work experience, I understood if I worked hard at something, I inevitably was going to get better at it.

Did you have a mentor?

I was lucky. Early on in my decision to become an illustrator, I reached out to this pretty well-known agent, Lilla Rogers. I knew someone who was represented by her, and they put in a good word for me. She was really instrumental in mentoring me. I think she appreciated that I was older and that I was pretty malleable. I had some basic skills and good ideas, I just needed more practice and someone to teach me the path.

What financial preparations did you have to make when you made the job transition?

I started by going part-time at my job at the nonprofit for six months. From there, I transitioned to freelancing for my former employer and also opening a retail gift store with my friend. That supplemented my art income for three years before I went whole-hog art 100 percent of the time. During those years, I finished paying off $60,000 of consumer debt that I had accumulated. I understood that for the short term I was going to have to make sacrifices and cut back on things like shopping and eating out and other luxuries.

How did you make your career as an artist financially viable?

I started putting work into the world before it was perfect or ready, just for the practice of doing it and understanding what resonated for people and what didn't. The first year as a full-time artist I made $50K. By that time, I had garnered a book illustration gig, my first book deal, and my Etsy shop was starting to make regular sales. That wasn't nearly what I was making when I left my career in the nonprofit world, which was closer to $100K a year, but I felt like I had accomplished something amazing. Incrementally over the years I've continued to increase my income. As you build your portfolio, more opportunities arrive.

SELL
YOUR

ART

*If you have been harboring hopes that your
artwork might be something someone wants to pay for,
take note of Lisa Congdon's top five pieces of advice.*

GET STARTED

My mantra has always been:
Begin anyhow. It's easier not to
do something than it is to do it,
especially because being creative
means being really vulnerable. You
need to push through that, show
up, and force yourself to practice
your art every day.

FIND A MARKET FOR YOUR
WORK ONLINE

There are multiple platforms where
you can teach and sell your art.
I teach classes on Creativebug,
CreativeLive, and Skillshare, plus
my own website. I also sell my work
on Etsy. Those options didn't exist
even ten or fifteen years ago.

3

LEVERAGE SOCIAL MEDIA

Buyers, art directors, and gallerists are finding new artists by looking online, so amp up your online presence. When I started, I remember feeling that I was just pimping my own work. It felt kind of yucky and then I realized, *This is what I have to do*. I approached marketing my work as something I was proud of and shared little bits of myself so people would also see the person behind the pictures. I grew an audience.

4

GET REPEAT BUSINESS

In order to keep your clients and get new ones, you have to make your current clients happy. You have to do good work and turn things in on time. The more you do that, the better chance you have at getting another assignment.

5

TAKE BREAKS

Leave time to regenerate creatively; otherwise you will burn out. Figure out how you can have a life outside of work, because then you have more to give. I found that being pickier about taking or not taking projects didn't impact my financial success at all. I am doing better than ever, and I feel happier.

WRITE
COMICS

FROM ▸

FINANCIAL
MANAGEMENT
CONSULTANT

TO ▸

COMIC BOOK
WRITER

> *"Being a creative person, as opposed to a businessperson, you care so much more."*

FALLING INTO A JOB I graduated from Harvard Business School, and I was totally unsure what was next. Everyone wants to find their passion, but if you don't know what that is, then you kind of just do what's available. I ended up in financial management consulting.

LAUNCHING AN ORIGINAL START-UP At a Harvard alumni event, my friend Georgia Lee had an idea for a start-up: comics for the YA set.

At the time, mainstream comics were so male-oriented; we saw our comics as more empowering with better role models for young girls and women.

ENTERING THE COMIC BOOK DIMENSION The idea was that Georgia would write the comics and do the creative side while I would handle the business side. I took an online writing class partly as a lark and partly just to understand the creative process. I put my two kids to bed, logged on, and it was all guys, all avid comic book fans. The whole class knew every comic book character, while I had to Wikipedia everything, thinking, *This is a terrible mistake.*

DISCOVERING A NEW TALENT One of the class assignments was to write a five-page story—beginning, middle, and end. It's actually very hard to write a complete story in five pages, and half of the class couldn't do it. I wrote mine, and the teacher loved it. Most new writers write too much, but my experience writing PowerPoint decks actually helped me be more succinct.

GOING FOR A NEW CAREER Georgia went on to direct a film and write for TV, but I still wanted to create comics. The year before, I'd had early-stage breast cancer, which makes you think, *What am I doing with my life?* I was married. I had health insurance and savings. I was in between consulting jobs. So I decided to go all in and try this comic book thing. I really loved it. I took art classes, writing classes, editing classes—every class you need in order to produce a book.

SELF-PUBLISHING I decided to write multiple short stories, one in every genre: sci-fi, superhero, fantasy, even romance. I figured the more stories I did, the more chance I had of at least one of them inspiring someone to hire me or buy my work. My anthologies were professionally produced. I had pull quotes and bar codes on the back. I worked with professional artists. I didn't want to look like an amateur.

BREAKING IN If you want to get into comics, know that it's incredibly hard. Everything is controlled by one distributor. They have a cash-up-front, no-refund policy, which means the comic stores have absolutely no incentive to buy anything other than what they know for sure their customer wants. To get in, you are going to have to self-publish, hustle at conventions, hand-sell, do your own PR, and try to drum up your own fan base online—all of which I did. It is very entrepreneurial.

ENTERING THE BIG LEAGUES A year after I published on my own, I had a chance to pitch to DC Comics. I got a story in called "So Blue." It was about an aging singer in Detroit who meets her younger rival, which is loosely based on Madonna meeting Taylor Swift. Then I did a Wonder Woman story, then Poison Ivy. Now I'm employed full-time writing comics for publishers.

STANDING OUT I write women who are smart and strong. I know it shouldn't be so unusual, but it is. Poison Ivy is a scientist, so I wrote her as smart and powerful. Red Sonja has been around since the seventies, so my take was to bring her into the present day and get her into some pants. I did it very subtly so nobody says, "Oh, my gosh, a feminist has taken over the series!" I put her on a motorcycle, and if she's on a motorcycle she needs pants.

MAKING COMICS MORE INCLUSIVE I try to find the core of the character and be consistent to that but do it in a way that opens them up to new readership. My big criticism of comics is they can be very stuck in terms of catering to older fans who belong to a certain demographic. So I feel my job as a newer writer, as a female writer, and as a writer of color is to open the story to new readers and still maintain that old readership. If I can do that, I'd consider it to be a huge success.

BEING A WOMAN IN A MALE-DOMINATED BUSINESS There are a lot of women who've entered and left the comic book world for a number of reasons. I decided I am not going to be run out of this industry. I am in, and I am going to stick with it.

HELPING OTHER WOMEN SUCCEED There has been a shift recently, and women have been a lot more visible. I'm making a huge effort to help. Once I realized I was the only woman on many panels, I knew that I had to reach out to the organizers, pitch a panel idea, and stack it full of women. There are women out there. They just aren't getting asked to do anything. There are a lot of female artists, fewer female writers, but that is changing.

APPRECIATING FANS I was on a panel talking about my job, and a woman came up to me and started crying, saying how important my presence as a woman meant to her. The comic fan base is really passionate about their characters and about this world. Being a creative person, as opposed to a businessperson, you care so much more. To have someone actually be affected by my work, it's like, *Wow! I am in a totally different world than before.*

BEFORE THEY WERE SUCCESSFUL NOVELISTS

Countless novelists had other careers before hitting the best-seller lists. Here are just a few.

TONI MORRISON
Editor

JOHN GRISHAM
Lawyer

KURT VONNEGUT
Owner of a car dealership

HARPER LEE
Airline ticketing agent

STEPHEN KING
High school janitor

JOHN GREEN
Chaplain

AMY BLOOM
Therapist

AMOR TOWLES
Investment banker

WRITE A NOVEL

Cristina Alger worked as a Goldman Sachs analyst,
then a corporate lawyer before her first novel, The Darlings,
became a hit. Currently working on her fourth book, Cristina
shares her top nine tips for would-be writers.

1

READ, READ, READ

As much as you can, across all genres and mediums. There is no greater teacher than a well-curated bookshelf.

2

ATTEND READINGS

Every time I have gone to listen to a writer talk about his or her work, I have come away with something valuable—from a book recommendation to a tip on structuring an outline.

3

DON'T WRITE FOR AN AUDIENCE

Write for yourself. If you want to read something, chances are someone else will, too.

4

FINISH A FULL DRAFT

Agents talk to a lot of aspiring novelists who have twenty or a hundred pages of what they believe is a masterpiece. And it very well might be—if it ever gets done. The words THE END get an agent's attention like nothing else. They signal that you have the grit required for the job.

5

DON'T LET PERFECT BE THE ENEMY OF GOOD

The first time I sent an agent a draft of my first novel, she said, "You know what we agents call most first drafts? Updrafts. Like something you throw up onto the page." I was horrified, but she actually meant it as a compliment. I had gotten the plot out there. It wasn't pretty, and it needed a lot of cleaning up, but that was okay.

6

COMMIT TO YOUR PROJECT

Carve out time in your calendar to write, as you would with any other commitment. Most writers have day jobs. They block out time before work, late at night, on weekends. Toni Morrison woke every morning at 5 a.m. before her job in publishing to write *The Bluest Eye*. It can be done. It just takes planning and follow-through.

7

REMEMBER THAT WRITING IS A BUSINESS

If you want to be a real writer, start thinking like one. Show up. Produce your work. Meet your own self-imposed deadlines. There will be many times when a sink full of dishes, a friend's birthday party, or a sick kid will call you away from your writing like a siren song. You mustn't give in. (Except with the sick kids.)

8

GROW A THICK SKIN

I thought I had one. I worked in finance for many years. I've been dressed down, yelled at, harassed, and embarrassed more times than I can count. And none of it compares to the hideous, horrible sting of a bad review or a nasty personal email from an irate reader. Writers get *crucified*. Publicly. It's awful. My agent once told me to look up the one-star Amazon reviews of a few books that we both agreed had been both critical and popular successes. And you know what? They exist. There are people who hate *The Age of Innocence*. Some think Tom Wolfe is a moron. Reading these things doesn't necessarily make me feel better about being called a talentless hack, but it is something of a salve. You can't please everyone. Especially on Amazon.

9

ALLOW YOURSELF TO FAIL

I know so many brilliant writers who have spent years working on projects that they later realized weren't worth showing to their agents. Some have published books that are absolute, total flops. But they all kept going. And thank goodness they did, because otherwise we wouldn't have all the beautiful books that have been written after failure. Don't think of those days as wasted ones. Think of them as time spent honing your craft.

FIND WORK THAT MAKES YOU
HAPPY

TESS FINNEGAN

FROM  **TO**

FEDERAL TRIAL ATTORNEY

FLORAL DESIGNER

IT TOOK ME TEN YEARS of thinking about switching gears before I did it. I wasn't miserable as a lawyer, but I knew there was something more that I wanted. I picked up a book by Danielle LaPorte called *The Desire Map*. Her whole thing is: it isn't about just setting goals and hitting them but focusing on how you want to feel when you are living your life. For me, it was a great way to get back into what I wanted to do. So I thought, *Okay, as a lawyer, how do I feel? I'm going a mile a minute. I am a paid fighter. I have all those stress illnesses.* It is an adversarial system, and it takes its toll.

As a trial attorney, you're fired up, and that adrenaline rush will take you pretty far for a long time, but what I really wanted was more sustainable. I wanted a job that gave me energy, not a job that drained me. I wanted to have a lot left over for my kids. I wanted that spark to come back to me, but I thought, *How am I ever going to do that?*

When my son was a year old, I resigned from the Department of Justice. My second child arrived a year later, and I soon attempted to reboot my career, looking for kinder, gentler law jobs. I had studied Latin, Greek, art, and archaeology in college, so I thought about art law. Then I had my third kid, and the bottom fell out. I didn't think I could do any lawyering until I got my brain back. I was getting all these legal opportunities, and I could not force myself to take them. I got an offer to edit legal textbooks, and I just saw a big pile of paper with black writing. I did some assistant lobbying work. I was all over the place trying to figure out what would give me lift-off.

I used to walk by a beautiful flower shop in Georgetown, and I would have this fantasy of me in the shop with a dog. I didn't think anything would ever come of it, but it never really went away, either. I don't know that I had any talent, but I loved flowers and was always making arrangements for my home and office.

During that time, I made a personal board of directors for myself with six friends who were entrepreneurs. I bounced three different ideas off of them: a travel app, a site to educate schools about kids with food allergies, and a flower shop. One friend's response was, "One of these is really expensive to launch. One can be sad. What do you know about flowers? Do you know how to run a business?" I told him I didn't, but I wanted to. He made it sound so simple: "Why don't you get a job at a flower shop? Don't tell anyone. Just see if you like it." I thought, *That's so easy! Why have I been overthinking this?*

So I ran with it. That day, I dropped two kids off at school and had the other kid on my hip when I walked into Ultra Violet Flowers and asked if they needed any help. It turned out the owner was happy for extra help. He asked if I was organized. Of course I was, having been an attorney. It was an example of hiring for attitude, not aptitude. I started the next week.

It was a great gig. I did everything. I swept the floor, organized glassware, and answered phones. The owner took me under his wing and taught me everything I know about the business and flowers. I started at $11 an hour; after nine months, I moved up to manager and got paid $16 an hour.

A year later the owner got a puppy, and I thought, *This is a dream come true: I am in this shop and arranging flowers with a dog.* But I also thought, *None of this is mine.* My babysitters were getting paid more than I was, and I was ready to start something for myself, so I launched Green Hydrangea Flowers. I now have a floral studio in my garage. I don't take any foot traffic, which is fine by me. When people pop in, they want to spend $30; when they call you, they want something bigger.

I still miss my lawyer paycheck. I can finally pay my mortgage, but it's been three years getting there. Maybe in a couple years, when the kids are closer to college, I'll have to make different choices, but for now it works.

So how do I feel? Being a florist is the polar opposite of litigating, where you are constantly under siege and everybody is angry. I am really joyful when I'm around flowers. I even love the prep work. I love being around beauty all the time. I especially love the currency of people saying "I love you" or "Thank you" or "Happy birthday." I love that we are creating this little system of joy and happiness and beauty through flowers.

CREATE SHOWSTOPPING INTERIORS

SUYSEL DEPEDRO CUNNINGHAM

FROM

ADVERTISING
ACCOUNT MANAGER

TO

INTERIOR
DESIGNER

"Had my dad known that there were careers like this, he could have made money."

CREATIVITY IS IN DESIGNER Suysel dePedro Cunningham's genes. Her father, Pedro, handmade dazzling wedding and Quinceañera dresses and costumes for performers—including the 1980s pop sensation Menudo. In her early teens, Suysel helped out, sewing pearls and sequins onto gowns and arranging flowers for events. Naturally,

> " *They say if you love it,* **THE MONEY WILL COME.** *For me, that was better than focusing only on income and being miserable.*

she gravitated toward design and color. "I was always around colorful fabrics, details, and trims," she recalls of her childhood in West Hartford, Connecticut. "There was never anything ivory, black, or basic in my life."

The problem was that although Suysel associated creativity with joy, she also related it to financial instability and eviction notices on their front door. "We moved all the time because my parents weren't paying rent. There was no opening bills and paying them. They would stack up," she explains. "In my mind, anything artistic and creative made no money. There was nobody who loved his job more than my father, and he couldn't make money off of it."

So after earning a scholarship to Tufts University in Boston, she took no art or design classes, focusing instead on economics, marketing, and international relations. She binged on shelter magazines and home design shows for fun, but her career ambitions were focused squarely on financial success. "I felt that in order to be successful, I had to go in a totally different direction than my father," Suysel explains. When Pedro passed away her sophomore year, Suysel had to deal with both grief and the pressure she felt to help her mother and brother financially upon graduation.

When thinking about career prospects, Suysel was intrigued by the thought of advertising. On paper, an account management role seemed like an ideal hybrid of left and right brain. After graduating in 1998, Suysel landed at Ogilvy & Mather, a top ad agency, at a salary of $28,000. To Suysel, it felt like a lot. Plus, it was enough to cover her own expenses and pay for her mother's car.

Suysel's tech savvy and Spanish skills proved to be an asset, landing her in the agency's budding interactive department. Over the next five years, she worked at three different agencies, increasing her salary with each job change. Despite her success, she didn't love the endless selling and putting out fires. She found herself envious of the creative team dreaming up campaigns. However, they were artists and writers, and she didn't see herself on that side of the business. It did open her eyes to the idea that financial stability and creativity could go hand in hand. "I remember thinking, *Had my dad known that there were careers like this, he could have made money.*"

Then, in 2002, the market crashed, and Suysel was laid off. Even though she didn't like her career, she went on autopilot, turning her attention to finding another advertising job. It was her sister-in-law who thought the time off could be a reset, asking, "What would you do if you could do anything?" For years, Suysel had been fascinated by the world of interior design, and for the first time, she revealed that being a decorator would be her dream job, but she didn't take the conversation seriously.

As fate would have it, the next day her sister-in-law received an email from a friend who was leaving her job as an assistant to the interior designer Markham Roberts. It was a personal assistant role, so the fact that she had no decorating experience wasn't an issue. Looking at Markham's gorgeous portfolio, she knew she wanted to spend her days in that world.

During the interview, Suysel made a strong case that her experience working with clients, pitching, selling, and managing would be an asset. She also had tech, web, and social media skills to bring to the table. "Markham had no website at that point, and he didn't think he needed one. I told him all the reasons he did. Plus I said, 'I'll also make your dinner reservations, I'm not above that.'" She was hired.

The job paid one-third of her previous salary. But with her severance, dipping into some savings, and health care benefits from her husband's job, the prospect didn't seem so terrifying. "I was married. I had more financial stability. I was really driven. I knew there was no going back to how I grew up," she says.

The ultimate goal was to set up her own interior design business, and learning from a top designer while getting paid seemed like a better choice than paying for interior design school and starting from scratch.

After five years working with Markham, Suysel launched her own firm. She teamed up with another former design assistant, Anne Maxwell Foster. "We bonded over how we both started our careers in advertising, hated it with a passion, and then landed in design," Anne says. After Suysel gave birth to her daughter, Cecilia, the pair spent six months envisioning and planning every aspect of their new firm. They worked on branding and social media, crafting their logo and website, and honing their style.

Without any official clients, they designed Suysel's house and used it to launch their site and social media pages. With thousands of followers on Twitter, they got noticed. Their first year in business, they were named interior designers to watch by *Traditional Home* and *Lonny* magazines. Eight years later, they are in-demand designers working on projects all over the country and designing their own line of fabrics for the Robert Allen Duralee Group, plus wall coverings for Hygge & West.

"They say if you love it, the money will come," says Suysel. "For me, that was better than focusing only on income and being miserable. Design is definitely my calling."

MAKE ART
FOR EVERYONE

DANIELLE MASTRION

FROM  **TO**

GRAPHIC
DESIGNER

MURALIST

I ALWAYS KNEW I WANTED to be a full-time artist, but there were detours. I went to Parsons and studied illustration, but the pressure of having student loans and paying rent meant I needed to get a full-time job right away. I began working as an artist's assistant in different studios and galleries. For about three years, I was doing everything from art handling to graphic design to general gallery assistant work.

I took advantage of those initial jobs. I learned how artwork is packaged for delivery, how to properly hang an exhibition, how to create promotional materials, how to organize a website, and how artwork is priced and sold. I watched curators speak with clients and buyers. The experience I got working those jobs was so important to my career now. That's the stuff they don't teach you in college.

With my graphic design experience, I eventually got a full-time job working at a small boutique ad agency in Midtown. The job was so demanding. I was working ten-, eleven-, twelve-hour days for about two years straight. Even though I was working in a creative field, I was still behind a computer. I wasn't drawing. I was hardly painting because of the demands of my day job. I felt like I might as well have been an accountant. The lack of freedom, the lack of being outside, plus sitting for twelve hours a day and not painting—it was causing constant anxiety attacks. After dealing with the stress for several months, I made the decision to quit.

I had family members who lived all over the country and went to go visit them. I didn't spend a lot of money, and I got a break from the New York hustle. I came back after a few months, and I started waitressing. I figured I could work at night and make some cash while I figured everything out.

I got an offer to work in another office as an illustrator, graphic designer, and T-shirt designer. I quit waitressing to give it a shot. It was an all-women-run company, and they wanted me to draw, paint, and illustrate their shirts. I loved the company, but I was still behind a desk. The company downsized and I got laid off from that job, which was a blessing. I never wanted to work in an office again.

I participated in more live painting events, like Art Battle, where artists complete a painting over the course of an evening. I also started going to mural events and meeting a community of working artists.

I started working as a tour guide while I navigated what I wanted to do in the art world. It was the best decision. I'm from New York and have always had an affinity for the city and its history. It is only a few hours a week, and the pay is really good for not too much time. I am now primarily painting, but I actually still lead tours because it's mentally challenging and I love the work.

Through my connections at the live painting events, I got invited to be in a couple of mural festivals. I gave it a try, and it was a fit. It checks off all the boxes: I'm painting. I'm outside. I'm interacting with people. I naturally paint large, and the scale and physicality of the work clicked with me. Painting murals has made me happier than I have ever been in my life. I found my niche.

When I started, it was a lot of local neighborhood or mural festivals, block parties, or me approaching a business and asking if I could paint their wall. I realized that every mural you put up is free advertising. I always leave my contact information on the wall with my signature. A lot of people started seeing my work, and that eventually led to a restaurant or a bar seeing the kind of work they would want in their establishment. Restaurant owners usually own two or three properties, and I would end up painting all of them.

Most of my mural work now is commission based, and a lot are city projects. I just did a huge mural for the New York Aquarium. I do a lot of restaurants, coffee shops, bars, and clubs. My favorite is the work I've done in Coney Island. It is the neighborhood that raised my mother, that raised me, and I'm finally getting to give back to the place that gave me so much

> 66
>
> *It checks off all the boxes: I'm painting. I'm outside. I'm interacting with people.*

happiness my entire life. As a New Yorker, getting to work at such historic institutions as Luna Park, Deno's Wonder Wheel, and the Cyclone is incredible.

I get contacted by a lot of human rights organizations, women's shelters, and anti–gun violence organizations that want murals done to spread their message. I painted a huge anti–gun violence mural on West 30th Street and Surf Avenue. That mural meant a lot to me because I know that gun violence unfortunately still plagues the neighborhood. Students from Art Start helped me paint, and a lot of the imagery came from my conversations with them.

Murals really connect with people and communities. What I love about public art is that it is available to everyone. A lot of people are afraid to go to galleries or museums. They think, *I don't belong there* or *I don't know anything about art*. Murals are a way to counter that mind-set and make artwork free and visible to everybody.

ROCK A CAREER
YOU HAVE NO EXPERIENCE IN

SIMON DOONAN

DAY JOB

—

RETAIL BRAND
AMBASSADOR
AND TV JUDGE

SIDE HUSTLE

—

WRITER

WITH HIS FLAIR FOR FASHION, dry sense of humor, and role as the creative ambassador for Barneys New York, it's no surprise that Simon Doonan is a bit of a media darling. He's also part of the media, penning clever, sharp, and witty books, plus essays for outlets such as Slate. Simon has a voice that's instantly recognizable (something all writers would kill for), which is why I was floored when he told me he hadn't written a word until he was 46. Here's how Simon went from not writing at all to writing best sellers.

What made you suddenly want to start writing at 46?

It all happened by chance. I was working on a picture book about my window-dressing career, and Nicholas Callaway, the publisher, asked me to write an intro. I spewed out all this stuff about my wacky childhood in England and how it gave me an idiosyncratic point of view, which then found its way into my wacky window designs. Nick called me screeching with enthusiasm: *Write more!*

What was the process of writing your first book like?

Working with a great editor, Antoinette White, I added loads more text to what had previously been just a straightforward picture book. *Confessions of a Window Dresser* got lots of attention. Madonna bought the movie rights, and my life sped off in this exciting, glam direction that I could never have predicted.

Did the book open new literary doors for you?

After *Confessions* came out in the late nineties, Peter Kaplan, the late, great editor of the *New York Observer*, called and asked me to write a regular style column. I impulsively said *Yaaasssss!* I began writing that column while I had a full-time corporate job at Barneys. I used to get up at 5:30 a.m. and bang away on my computer and then skip off to work. I had no idea where it would lead, but I was happy to have this new, unexpected creative outlet. I saw writing as a fresh way to express myself.

Peter Kaplan was known for mentoring many writers. What did you learn from working with him?

Before I started on my column, Peter asked me to write a couple of book reviews. He gave me good advice: "The key to writing a great book review is to write about anything except the book." I blathered on about myself, which is what I do most of the time when I write.

How did your writing career evolve?

I wrote the weekly *Observer* column for ten years. And then, when all the websites started arriving, I switched to Slate.com. I once wrote an op-ed for the *New York Times*. They rewrote it and took out all the funny bits. This is when I realized that I was very much a humor writer and that there was no point in writing for a humorless publication, even if it was the *New York Times*. Also, when the *Times* reviewed my book *Nasty* (renamed *Beautiful People* after it was turned into a BBC TV show), they described me as "foppish and superficial." My husband, Jonathan Adler, and I had a good laugh about that. All I ever wanted was to be foppish and superficial. It felt like a coronation!

It takes a certain amount of guts to write a piece and then put it out into the world for consumption/criticism. Were you ever nervous about that aspect of writing?

The main lesson I learned from my gritty childhood is that you cannot worry too much about what other people think. When I was a teenager, it was illegal to be gay and people were openly hostile to gay people. My dad warned me that gay people ended up in prison, a mental hospital, or they killed themselves. So if you were gay, you had to learn to value yourself and not worry about what other people thought. As a result, my generation of gays is very tough and resilient.

With writing, I never felt precious about it. I always approached writing as a J-O-B. I have working-class attitudes about productivity and work. And getting paid. Plus, designing windows for Barneys has made me thick-skinned. Every week you unfurl your creativity to the world and you get instant feedback. You can stand outside the window and listen to all this brutal criticism. It's great practice for being a writer.

Did writing humor come naturally to you?

I always had a very clear sense of the kind of writing that worked for me: cheeky and irreverent is my brand. I try to write the kind of stuff that I would want to read. In England my throwaway style is a dime a dozen (my favorites are Deborah Ross and Julie Burchill). But in the USA I am more of a one-off. American culture is very playful—until it gets into print. Then everything can get very earnest. The Brits are the opposite. The culture is very formal, but the writing styles, even in posh newspapers, tend to be very informal.

You've published seven books, all while doing your day job at Barneys. How have your two careers played off each other?

My two careers are symbiotic. I am 65 years old. I have spent most of that time in fashion and retail, and I am very grateful to retail and all of the people who have employed me and put a roof over my head! I cannot think of anything worse than being stuck at home writing for my entire adult life. I need the contact high from working and collaborating. If my writer pals are having a rough time, I always tell them to go get a part-time job at Home Depot. Retail will get you out of the house and blow away the cobwebs! If Virginia Woolf had taken a part-time job at the Harrods cheese counter, I am sure it would have helped salvage her mental health.

What advice do you have for aspiring writers?

If writing makes you unhappy, and you procrastinate or you have to drink Scotch in order to get going—then try something else. Writing should make you happy.

STAR IN YOUR
OWN SHOW

JILL KARGMAN

FROM — ▶

NOVELIST

TO — ▶

PRODUCER,
WRITER, AND
ACTRESS

I WAS ALWAYS IN A PLAY when I was in college. I loved acting. I remember when I took my last bow of my last show my senior year, I thought, *This is so sad, I'm never going to act again.* It just didn't even occur to me to pursue it. I didn't look like other actresses. I'm pale and spooky-looking, and everyone in Hollywood is blond, tits on sticks. I also couldn't imagine being a hostess in a restaurant waiting for that audition call. That would have stressed me out so much. I'm not wired for the lifestyle of rejection on a constant basis.

So I said good-bye to all that and became a writer. I just figured writing was more fair: it's all about your voice, not how you look. I started as an intern at *Harper's Bazaar* and then went on to be an assistant editor at *Interview.* Even though I was a magazine writer

and it sounds creative, it was more like servitude: fetching coffee and booking travel. But I did get to write. Even if I had a tiny two-hundred-word story in the front of the book, I had a byline and I felt like I was making progress. Every tear sheet that I could add to my portfolio was something.

The female bosses I had at the time didn't have personal lives; it was all about work. I knew that I wanted to have children, so it wasn't a long-term place for me. I wanted to transition into writing books and screenplays.

I wrote a movie called *Intern* about my experiences working in fashion with my writing partner at the time, Carrie Karasyov. It's really just an extension of what I had been doing, writing about the fashion and media world. Carrie and I would meet up with friends at the Odeon, and everyone was bitching about their jobs. We were telling these stories, and everyone would say, "You have to write this down. You can't make this stuff up." We didn't take a class. I felt like I'd seen so many movies, so I could do it. With a partner the dialogue comes so easily because you're just telling stories and developing it out loud together.

From there, I got into writing for MTV as a freelancer in the MTV News and Docs department. I wrote voiceovers for pop culture comedy shows such as *So Five Minutes Ago*. Then I got pregnant, and MTV just stopped calling me. Meanwhile, these are 36-, 37-year-olds with vintage Clash T-shirts and messenger bags; they're like rejuveniles. But I showed up very pregnant, and they all started freaking out. I was like, "Wait, I'm 28, I'm much younger than you guys!" But pregnancy meant I wasn't edgy.

I went back to writing books. Carrie and I had written a screenplay about a Park Avenue building called *The Right Address*. We sent it to our agent, and she said, "I have good news and bad news. The good news is, I absolutely loved it. But it's too esoteric and too New Yorky." I said, "That's absurd, look at *Sex and the City*." But that was a book first and had a built-in following before it was a show. So I said, "Let's write it as a book."

That started my career as a book writer. I've been a writer all along; it's just been in different mediums. I had two more kids in rapid succession, and with three kids under four I just couldn't leave them to go to LA and pitch TV shows. It just felt like a waste of time. Hollywood buys, like, five times as many properties as they tend to produce. With books, if you get a book deal, it's going to be published. I felt like if I'm going to take time away from my kids and do work, it might as well see the light of day.

I wrote a collection of essays called *Sometimes I Feel Like a Nut*, and something clicked with me. I was like, *This is my voice!* I told my editor I wanted to write another essay collection, and she said no. The rejection really changed my life for the better. They wanted another novel because they made more money with my novels than my essays. After writing something that felt more real, I couldn't go back. I didn't want to whore myself out.

A friend of mine told me about a copywriting job at Ogilvy. I was really happy to be in an office again after all those years as a mother. It was only two or three days a week, and I did a lot of "female" accounts, whether it was sanitary napkins or a diaper that catches your pee when you sneeze or whatever. It was purely for the money, but I felt like it was exercising my brain, and I needed that.

A year later my bosses there said, "You're funny, you should be on TV." I was like, "All right, I'll get right on that!" They said, "No, really, we can help you make a sizzle reel." And we totally did. Guerrilla style.

> **"**
> *People were like, "You haven't acted in, like, twenty years?" And I said,* **"NO, BUT I GOT THIS!"**

We basically pitched a late-night show that would air in the morning. It was called *Wake the F- Up.* It didn't have the attitude of the morning shows that are so perky. We sent it out and nobody bought it, but I got a lot of meetings. I met with Andy Cohen and Lara Spotts at Bravo, who said they thought I would be great for a reality show. And I said, "I'm so flattered, but I could never have a camera up my sphincter." With all due respect to all of the franchises they have, that's not for me.

I told them I would love to write a scripted show for them because I'd heard they were going into scripted. I sent them my novel *Momzillas* and my essays. They thought that there could be a show of both of those in a blender. So we had more meetings where we developed *Odd Mom Out*.

Bravo was the one that said it: "We think you should be on camera. We think you have a specific voice and a way of performing it." I was excited. I felt like I could totally do it in my sleep. We shot a pilot, and the rest is history.

It was such a weird thing because I was 39 years old and we're shooting the first day and people were like, "You haven't acted in, like, twenty years?" And I said, "No, but I got this!" I love the collaborative aspect of television—having writers, actors, and directors to giggle with all day. Even when we are exhausted, we stop and say, "Can you believe we are getting paid for this?"

It's hilarious to switch professions at 40. I think it's even funnier that I picked the profession that is the most ageist of all. But with wrinkles come experience and more to funnel into performing. Also, at 22 I would have been worried about stupid stuff like the circumference of my thighs, whereas now I don't even think about that. I would definitely do more acting. But when people ask, "What do you do?" I say I'm a writer.

2

LAUNCH
YOUR OWN
BUSINESS

---

*Become a Social Media Guru /
Invent Something /
Start a New Brand / Code Your Way to a Career /
Find a Gap in the Market*

HOW HAS NO ONE ELSE THOUGHT OF THIS? This is going to be your ticket to greatness. It's a fresh angle, an overlooked opportunity, a pioneering concept. No more cubicles. You are going to be the one running things, bringing in capital, taking it national. Maybe global.

Now you just have to figure out how to make it happen.

Can you quit your job? How much money will you need to get started? What does a business plan even look like? Do you need an MBA? How do you launch a website? Can you teach yourself to code?

Once you dive into what it takes to start a business, you will understand why the idea is the easy part. The dreamers get separated from the doers pretty quickly. Taking it to profitability is the next challenge. Then you need to keep it going.

This chapter features an intrepid group of business owners. When everyone else was retiring, they were just getting started. When no one was offering funding, they figured out how to stop waiting on other people and just start. When they kept failing, they used it as an impetus to launch into an entirely new career.

They went over obstacle after obstacle to launch their ideas.

You're next.

BECOME A
SOCIAL MEDIA
GURU

LEONARD KIM

FROM ▸

SHOE
SALESMAN

TO ▸

SOCIAL MEDIA
AND PERSONAL
BRANDING
SPECIALIST

*"I thought people were going to call me a loser. . . .
Instead they were like, 'You're such an inspiration!'"*

FROM THE OUTSIDE, the start-up world sounds like a good bet. Hit on a great idea, and you can score millions of dollars in funding, create a life-changing product, and cash out with a few million in the bank. The reality, however, is that 60 percent of all start-ups fail. The Los Angeles–based digital media expert Leonard Kim knows this only too well. After working as a shoe salesman at Macy's, Leonard went the start-up route to try to make money quickly, partly to impress a girl-friend who wanted him to earn six figures.

Leonard's early forays into start-ups were wildly unsuccessful. A loan start-up and a music start-up both went bankrupt. He moved on to positions at a real estate company and an investment fund, both of which went bust, too. Along the way the girlfriend he was trying to woo dumped him. The business failures meant he couldn't pay his bills; he was evicted from his apartment and moved in with his grandmother.

"The first time I failed at something, it really didn't hit me. The second time, I started getting a little scared. The third time, it was panic attacks. After that it just became very, very discouraging. I kind of gave up. I didn't really want to try anymore," says Leonard. "What forced me to finally do something was my grandma yelling at me to find a job."

Leonard joined another underfunded start-up that only paid him $2,300 over nine months. Realizing his job wasn't going anywhere and that he couldn't live with his grandmother forever (he was too embar-rassed to even date), he borrowed a few hundred dollars from a friend and moved to Los Angeles to live on a friend's sofa and start over.

With a résumé that was littered with bankrupt companies, Leonard got no results from hundreds of queries. Desperate, he asked a close friend, Deinis Matos, to hire him to work at American Honda Motor Company in an entry-level customer service role for $16 an hour. For the next few years, he spent no additional money, skipping lunch most days. He invested what income he could to have a small cushion if things went wrong again.

The turning point came when a colleague shared a post from the entrepreneur James Altucher on Quora. The author's personal story of career challenges and hurdles resonated with Leonard. "He was just like me, except he made a lot more money than I did, and he lost a lot more money," explains Leonard. "A lot of his content is about going out there and doing something. So I tried that and wrote my first post."

Leonard started writing about his failed attempts at success. "I didn't think it would amount to anything. It was just me writing because I had all these things I needed to let out. I wanted to tell people how to prevent the same mistakes I made. But it all started when I wrote about how horrible the things in my life were going." His articles soon started being shared, and he received hundreds of encouraging comments. The attention and approval inspired him to keep going, and he began writing two to four times a day.

Within six months Leonard's articles had been read two million times. He realized that the more candid he was about his failures, the more his story resonated with his readers. "There was no intent of being inspirational. I thought people were going to call me a loser, mock me, ridicule me," admits Leonard. "Instead they were like, 'You're such an inspiration! I can't believe you're sharing this.'"

Not only did the posts provide Leonard with a large audience, but they connected him with a whole new network. "I went from being this guy who really only knew salespeople to this guy who was able to connect with lawyers, Ivy Leaguers, consultants at McKinsey & Co., investment bankers—all these successful people." After a year and a half, his articles had been read ten million times and he had more than 20,000 followers on Quora.

Leonard began thinking of ways to monetize his newfound skills and audience. He launched a website to showcase his writing and present himself as an expert. He offered free social media consulting and wrote articles to build up a portfolio. After a few months, he was able to get paid to write content for companies, anywhere from $250 to a few thousand dollars, depending on the assignment. His growing reputation as a writer opened up the opportunity to contribute his expertise to publications such as *Inc.*, *Entrepreneur*, and the *Huffington Post*.

To get a day job that mirrored his newfound skills, Leonard applied to the University of Southern California to manage the social media following for Keck Medicine of USC. It paid almost three times as much as his salary at Honda and officially boosted his credibility as a social media guru. In a little over a year, Leonard took its Twitter following from 10,000 to 230,000.

Given that higher social media numbers can make experts look more legitimate, help businesses increase sales, and boost the reach of influencers, Leonard found plenty of clients who wanted to learn the secrets to digital success. Leonard and his business partner, Ryan

---

HOW I GOT HERE

Seven jobs Leonard Kim failed at before he became a social media whiz

Sold burned CDs for $250 a week–
UNTIL CD BURNER BROKE.

Was a marketer at a failed music start-up–
LOST ALL HIS MONEY.

Was a sales manager at a real estate company–
BEFORE IT WENT BANKRUPT.

Worked in investor relations at an investment fund–
BEFORE IT WENT BANKRUPT.

Worked at a start-up doing lead generation for loan modifications, credit repair–
BEFORE IT WENT BANKRUPT.

Was hired to work as a financial adviser, contingent on passing a life insurance test–
WITH NO MONEY SAVED TO PAY FOR THE TEST.

Worked as a telemarketer/fund-raiser to afford the life insurance test–
FAILED THE TEST.

Foland, set up an online course and launched InfluenceTree. "We teach people how to build their brand, get featured in publications, and grow their social media following," explains Leonard.

Leonard consults with clients such as venture capitalists, executives, and best-selling authors, along with regular people who are trying to rise up the ranks in more standard careers.

"Who needs a personal brand? It's more like who *doesn't* need one," he says. "A personal brand is really an extension of who you are—both digitally and in real life. With how seamless the internet is becoming to the real world, it's becoming a lot more important that who you are online reflects who you are in real life."

While his career skyrocketed, Leonard experienced heartbreak a few more times, but with both love and work, he realized that sometimes you have to go through failures to find the right fit. "I work with people that I never imagined working with and I really like what I do," says Leonard, before adding, "I also just got married to the woman of my dreams."

LAUNCH A
START-UP

KATIE WARNER JOHNSON

FROM
—
DANCER AND
FITNESS
INSTRUCTOR

TO
—
COFOUNDER
AND CEO OF AN
ACTIVEWEAR
BRAND

"If I had gone to business school, I never would have started this company."

IN 2011, KATIE WAS a professional dancer and fitness instructor looking for a fresh start. "My job wasn't sustainable," Katie explains. "All that hard work on my body had caught up with me. I was getting injured. The doors were starting to close by nature of my age. I had to make an adjustment quickly."

Katie, a Harvard grad, had her sights set on launching a tech start-up. "I was seeing people finding loopholes that big companies

weren't seeing," she explains. "They would have an idea, turn it into a product that acquired hundreds of thousands of customers, then sell that company and make money. It was compelling." She wanted to focus her business in the fitness space—it was an industry and clientele she knew incredibly well from her years as an instructor.

Along with two friends, Katie went to a weekend start-up event in San Francisco to fast-track their idea—to create the Yelp of fitness—into a business plan. The event was a portal to an entirely new world and introduced Katie to countless tech company founders, some of whom got their start through accelerator programs. "I got to see this path to creating a company, what that track looked like," she says. "It was key. I believe you have to see it to become it."

Katie and her partners applied to several accelerators, but without a cofounder with tech experience, it was a challenge to get into a program. They were eventually accepted by StartEngine in Los

Angeles. The program provided $30,000 in funding and the ability to refine their concept. "It gave us the permission to sit in an office for four months, think of ideas, and try to push something to a viable product at the end. It made us focus and taught us nimbleness. If I had gone to business school, I never would have started this company." Even after graduating from the program, they pivoted their concept several times before hitting on the right one. They landed it after noticing that there was an uptick in apparel vendors outside of Nike and Lululemon that didn't have distribution beyond mom-and-pop shops.

In 2013, Katie and her cofounder, Caroline Gogolak, launched a hybrid marketplace-ecommerce-retailer for activewear that they called Carbon38. Katie says the toughest part of building a business was raising capital. She raised the first $15 million in $25,000 increments. "It was a lot of meetings," she says. "It takes stamina. It takes a really clear commitment to what you are trying to do. Institutional investors hear so many pitches a day, and you need to figure out how to cut through that noise and convince them that what you're building is worthwhile and will give them a return."

Today Katie is running Carbon38 on her own, and the company has expanded beyond athletic wear into work and evening clothes made with high-performance fabrics. Foot Locker just invested $15 million in a minority stake. Carbon38 boutiques have opened within select Neiman Marcus stores, along with the first brick-and-mortar stores in Bridgehampton, New York, and Pacific Palisades, California. "We might not be saving the world with spandex, but if I can make the lives of my team, my customers, and our community better in some small way every day, that is an opportunity and responsibility I shoulder with pride."

GET YOUR IDEA OUT THERE

TIFFANY PHAM

FROM

DIRECTOR
OF BUSINESS
DEVELOPMENT
FOR A TELEVISION
NETWORK

TO

FOUNDER
AND
CEO OF A MOBILE
APP AND PLATFORM
FOR WOMEN

WHEN I WAS 27, I was listed on *Forbes*'s "30 Under 30" list. Being on the *Forbes* list caught the attention of many young women, and they started to write me letters asking for advice. After receiving my advice, they would often write me back and say my letter had changed their life: they'd gotten an opportunity they didn't think was possible or an interview or a promotion. Instead of sharing all of this advice one-on-one, I thought, *Why not create a platform for millions of young women to be able to share our ideas, our struggles, and our career opportunities?* That was how my idea for Mogul began.

I didn't have money to hire someone to help me launch the site. So I thought I could teach myself how to code and build the platform myself. It took me a couple of months to create the first version of Mogul. I basically didn't sleep.

The first few weeks were literally spent figuring out what software to download. I bought books on coding, but I couldn't get through them. My brother told me about *Ruby on Rails Tutorial* by Michael Hartl. It was more step-by-step and action-oriented, which made sense to me. Once I learned, I couldn't wait to get home and code. Coding changed my life because it was ultimately the last facet of the business that I needed to learn to launch the app.

Within a week of launching Mogul, it exploded, reaching a million people. When we got to that level that quickly, it was so unexpected. I completed all other jobs and side hustles to focus on it. I remember working 24/7 to support all of our users. For three months I was doing everything: designing, coding the features, launching partnerships, doing distribution and marketing. That was when I realized I couldn't handle it as one person.

> "
> *I've learned it is better to* **GET THINGS OUT THERE** *and get them toward perfection* **LATER**.

I reached out to a friend, who introduced me to one of his advisers at his company. I ended up pitching Mogul for the very first time to that adviser, Will Bunker, a cofounder of Match.com. For the very first pitch you do, you should probably practice in advance on someone other than a major veteran of the industry. Once I got the introduction, though, I didn't have time to practice. I threw myself into the fire. I've learned it is better to get things out there and get them toward perfection later. Will said yes and came on board as an investor and adviser. Once I had my first yes, a couple more incredible founders and innovators joined and I was able to raise millions of dollars in funding.

My advice to anyone wanting to launch a technology business is to go ahead and mock up your prototypes in order to put your idea out there. Just get started, always, and move toward perfection over time. Don't worry about the mistakes you may make along the way. You will get there.

INVENT
SOMETHING

DAY JOB

—

RETAIL SALES ASSOCIATE

SIDE GIG

—

INVENTOR

"I tell people, when sliced bread came out, it took ten years to catch on because people are reluctant to make changes."

JEFFREY NASH ALWAYS WANTED to have his own business, but the right idea didn't come along until he was 56. At that point, he had served in the marines, worked for General Electric, sold business machines, and spent more than twenty years selling men's clothing. "For years, I looked for something I could call my own," he says.

The big idea struck in 2011, when he was at his granddaughter's soccer game. Jeffrey noticed a mother hunched over, holding onto her baby's hands, trying to teach her to walk; it looked wildly uncomfortable. He immediately envisioned a contraption that would allow parents to stand up while helping babies take their first steps.

Jeffrey went straight to a tailor to create a prototype. His testers? The babies of friends and retail customers. "I would say to parents, 'Try it. I want to hear what you have to say. Is it easy to use? Is it something you would purchase?'" Over three months, he went through five different prototypes using their feedback to finesse the design and materials.

The next step was getting the Juppy onto store shelves. Over a three-week vacation, he went to children's stores in LA and San Diego, walking in and pitching to the store manager on the spot. He made $12,000. It was the confirmation he needed that he was on to something big.

> "
> *I think*
> *we are*
> AHEAD
> OF OUR
> TIME.

To launch, Jeffrey quit his sales job and invested $35,000 of his savings plus $9,000 from family and friends. Amazon proved to be a great initial outlet, selling $80,000 worth of product in the first year, with the best year at $170,000. Other manufacturers tried to copy the Juppy, but thanks to a utility patent, he was able to fight off competitors.

After three years of the financial highs and lows of launching a new product, Jeffrey wanted a more stable income. He returned to his job in clothing sales and now works on the Juppy on the side. "I think we are ahead of our time. I tell people, when sliced bread came out, it took ten years to catch on because people are reluctant to make changes." He believes that when they do make the change, there is no going back. "When we are featured on CNN or the *New York Times*, sales go off the chain, so that tells me that most of my problem is there are a lot of people who don't know about the Juppy. Eventually they will."

Jeffrey admits that working two jobs can be taxing. He is up by 5 a.m., packaging the sales from the day before, working on tweaking Google AdWords, and posting on social media. He then heads to his retail job at 9 a.m. After a full day of work, he turns his attention to increasing product sales. "I'm coming up on my sixty-fourth birthday, and I have days when it is somewhat overwhelming to try to do everything we need to do. So I counter that with making sure I get exercise. I meditate."

Jeffrey is optimistic about the future and is happy to stay on the roller-coaster ride of owning his own business. "I like the fact that you are constantly learning something new. You are constantly having to deal with failure, which I think is wonderful! You need to embrace adversity. You need to get used to it and understand that not every day is going to be a good day, but also not every day is going to be a bad day, it's just life," he says. "You just never know what the next email is going to bring."

START A NEW
BRAND
WHEN EVERYONE ELSE IS RETIRING

TRICIA CUSDEN

FROM

MANAGEMENT
TRAINER

TO

BEAUTY BRAND
FOUNDER

PREVIOUS GIG I became a management trainer in 1986, and I loved it from day one. I landed an interview through a friend's husband, and then did a weeklong course to assess my capabilities. I did very well, and they offered me a job. I developed a three-day course called Personal Power and Influencing, which was designed to help people become better able to manage their work relationships and understand how their behaviors impact others.

AN UNEXPECTED DETOUR My granddaughter India was born in January 2012 and soon after was diagnosed with a rare chromosomal abnormality. I was needed immediately to help care for her two-year-old sister, Freya, as my daughter, Suzy, needed to stay at India's bedside. It was clear that I could no longer work with clients, so I turned down all offers of work for almost a year. By October, however, India was able to go home and be supported by a team of caregivers. I still helped out when needed, but things began to return to a more normal routine.

RETIREMENT? NO, THANK YOU As India's life propelled me into withdrawal from paid work, I was very much in need of a new challenge. I was 65 and spending a lot of time watching daytime TV and thinking *I can't just watch TV for the next thirty years!* I felt that my life lacked purpose and direction. I had lost contact with all my clients during the year that India was in the hospital, and at my age I didn't want to start all over from scratch trying to create new contacts. I wanted to try something new and different.

A BUSINESS IDEA BORN OUT OF FRUSTRATION I was finding it difficult to source makeup that worked well on my older face. I kept thinking that there must be other older women who felt as frustrated as I did, who would like to be offered some great products that would really work and help them look incredible. I decided to launch Look Fabulous Forever to create and sell the products I wanted.

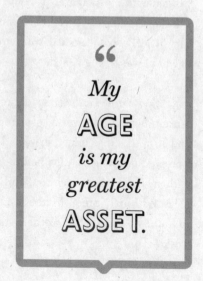

"
My
AGE
is my
greatest
ASSET.

WHAT THE MAJOR BEAUTY BRANDS DON'T GET There is nothing in a store likely to make older women feel comfortable about a beauty purchase. The sales assistants are all invariably young and heavily made up in a way that would look awful on an older face. The beauty brands don't accept the fact that older faces are different from younger ones. Older faces are never used for advertising makeup. Recently, YSL named 25-year-old Cara Delevingne as its face of anti-aging. Need I say more?

PREPARING TO LAUNCH I used £40,000 [about $53,000] to start. I risked only an amount I could afford so that if it failed, I would not be materially affected. I set about finding a UK-based cosmetic manufacturer that would be able to formulate the makeup in the way I was suggesting. I literally googled "UK cosmetic manufacturers," and I found one that looked promising and rang them up. The boss, Alan, was immediately enthusiastic about my idea and did me the enormous favor of making only two hundred of each product at a time. Now we are one of his best customers. To design packaging and create a logo, I worked with the daughter-in-law of a friend who is a graphic designer. The photographer was a contact from a teacher I knew and charged me very little. People seemed to warm to the idea and were very supportive of what I was trying to achieve.

FREE MARKETING In the first year of business, YouTube was the single most important way we had of attracting customers to our website. We had no marketing budget, so we had to use free social media platforms. I created two videos, plus before-and-after makeover photographs, with my friends as models to show how the makeup transformed older faces. Within four months, the two YouTube videos were getting 1,000 to 1,500 views a day, and orders started to come in from all over the world.

THE FINANCIAL REALITY I took no salary for two years and plowed every penny back into the business. Gradually the income grew so that we could afford higher overheads for things such as more staff and office space. We also attracted investment, and this has facilitated our very fast growth to current total profits in excess of £2 million [around $2.6 million]. Total profits in the first full year (2014) were £100,000.

REAL WOMEN. NO BOTOX. We have a very high repeat-customer rate, which shows how much older women love the effect of the makeup. We use only real older women who have not had work done, including fillers and Botox. We never airbrush our images. This makes us stand out in an industry that cannot come to terms with an aging face and wants us all to chase youthfulness at any cost.

AGE IS AN ADVANTAGE I am my target customer, so I know how to talk to older women without being patronizing. When I appear on TV or speak on the radio, my voice and face are authentic, and my age is my greatest asset. The business has rejuvenated me and given me a great sense of purpose. I'm really passionate about confronting ageism in society and becoming a voice for older women everywhere who are feeling invisible, marginalized, and ignored.

CODE
YOUR WAY TO A CAREER

JON DENG

FROM

US ARMY
OFFICER

TO

SOFTWARE
ENGINEER

AFTER FOUR YEARS IN the US Army as a platoon leader and field artillery officer, Jon Deng started thinking about his next move. He became intrigued with the possibilities of tech after he successfully taught himself the coding language Python to help process intelligence data in seconds rather than hours. Impressed by what he could accomplish on his own, he decided to get additional training to see if it could lead to a career in tech.

Jon applied to a programming bootcamp called Hack Reactor. Based in San Francisco, it offers an intensive twelve-week remote online course. During his last three months in the army, Jon was able to do the course around his work thanks to a manager who supported his effort and gave him minimal duties.

Even though the class was remote, Jon appreciated the camaraderie. "When you teach yourself, it's hard to keep motivated, get feedback, and know how you're doing, so you can quickly fall off," he explains. "It's a lot easier to be committed to something when you have a group of people who all are demonstrating that same level of commitment and you're able to bounce ideas off of them and collaborate together."

According to Glassdoor, the average starting salary for software engineers is around $128,000. The high salary makes the career more appealing—and more competitive. Though a coding certificate from Hack Reactor will prove you can do the work, it isn't a guarantee you will get hired. "You don't graduate, then click 'Apply' and land your dream job. In my experience, there was a lot of hustling and networking and trying to make different opportunities work by reaching out to people who I found online on sites like Medium, Hacker News, and Product Hunt."

Jon got his first software engineering job because a friend heard that he was interested in programming, and her employer, Snapchat, ended up hiring him as a software engineer. He is now working at Credit Karma, creating a financial assistant that allows people to monitor the financial health of their second-biggest asset, their car. "The best part of my job is seeing the results of my work," he says. "When I create a new feature, I can see how it works immediately and see on our analytics tools how thousands of people are using the feature that I built—that's really rewarding."

LAND A JOB IN

TECH

Timur Meyster, a project manager turned software engineer,
his brother, Artur, and a friend, Ruben Harris, all broke into tech from
other fields. After countless friends asked them how, they launched
the podcast Breaking Into Startups to highlight stories of people who had
broken into tech from nontraditional backgrounds. Here, Timur shares
their answers to the top five questions they are frequently asked:

How can someone break in if they haven't been coding since age 12?

Starting out, I read stories of guys like Elon Musk, who built games at age 11, and I almost felt like I'd missed my shot. However, that couldn't be further from the truth. When people look at Mark Zuckerberg, they see him as a child prodigy. To an outsider, it might appear that he has single-handedly built Facebook. However, Mark has an army of engineers, designers, and product managers who all worked together in building it. What they don't see is someone from their neighborhood who is now working on Facebook's engineering team, earning a great salary, contributing to the product, and enjoying all of the nice perks. Today, Facebook probably has over 10,000 people working on its products.

What opportunities are there at tech companies for people who don't code?

There are a lot of jobs in sales, customer service, operations, recruiting, and data analytics that are available to people who are breaking into their first role in tech. The skills involved in these roles lean more on the soft skills of that individual, and you're able to add value to a start-up from day one.

What courses are good if someone wants to learn to code? How can you go through a bootcamp without spending a lot of money?

Courses like Codecademy, Treehouse, and Code School do a good job teaching new coders the fundamentals in a fun, engaging way. Some bootcamps offer scholarships, while others like

App Academy and Grace Hopper Academy offer deferred tuition that you can pay back once you get a job. Programs like Climb and Skills offer a loan that covers tuition and living expenses up to $25,000 if you're able to get accepted into one of the top bootcamps. It's a great way to get a bridge loan while you're transitioning careers, as most people make about six figures after they do a top coding bootcamp.

How can you land a tech job if you don't know anyone in the business?

Research roles that you might find interesting. Then go on LinkedIn and find twenty people who do those jobs and email them with personalized messages. Tell them you admire their success and would like to talk to see how they got to where they are today. Most jobs are not found online. If you send out enough of these personalized messages and connect, you'll create a small network of people in tech who can either refer you to the company that they work at or connect you with someone else in tech who is hiring.

If you are coming to tech from a different field, how can you pitch yourself successfully to land the job?

It's all about how you tell your story. When people transition into a new career they sometimes think that they don't have a lot to offer except their drive. So they might say to an interviewer, "If you give me a shot, I'll prove to you I can do it." This is the wrong mind-set and something you should never do. By saying that, what it basically sounds like is you don't have relevant experience and you would need mentorship before you can contribute and make an impact on their team. You also haven't told them what you've done in the past that produced results or highlighted your accomplishments.

If you were a teacher and you're applying for a product management role, you could emphasize managing a classroom of eleven-year-olds and your thought process behind designing a class plan. When designing software, you'll use a similar skill set or framework and just apply it to software. Think of examples from your life where you used a skill set needed for the job and share those stories.

FIND A
GAP
IN THE MARKET

GE WANG

FROM

LAWYER

TO

OWNER OF
A BESPOKE
MENSWEAR
BUSINESS

> *"While the world goes more digital, we are going to do it analog. We're going to do it the classical way, the right way."*

IT WAS HIS FATHER'S total lack of interest in fashion that sparked Ge Wang's fascination with clothing. "My dad was a lawyer, but he would go to work in an ill-fitting suit. He never really dressed the part," Ge explains. "So, starting in law school, I kind of made it my mission to dress up."

Despite Ge's efforts to look sharp while clocking in as a real estate lawyer in Chicago, he wasn't impressed with what was available, even when he splurged on a custom suit from a top local tailor. "I was pretty in shape, and I thought, *Why don't I look like these guys in magazines?*" he jokes. So on his next trip to visit relatives in Beijing, a city that boasts some of the world's top tailors, Ge had a suit made. Not only did the young lawyer notice the difference, his friends did, too—and they wanted their own. Knowing he could offer his friends a better-fitting suit at a lower price than what was available in Chicago, an idea for a side business was born. He sold thirty suits his first year, all while clocking in at his day job.

Ge admits he mistakenly thought selling suits would be fairly simple. He figured he just had to learn how to measure, get some sample fabrics, and work with a tailor overseas. He was wrong. "I thought there wasn't much to it, especially the measuring, but that alone is super in-depth. A lot of it is human anatomy, understanding how the body works."

Business grew quickly by word of mouth, and after two years of working from his apartment, he had to make some decisions. "I was half-assing both things, and I had to choose one or the other. I really liked this new gig a lot more, so I made the choice to leave law," says Ge, who launched ESQ Clothing in 2012. "A few years ago, if you'd told me I would be running a clothing business, I would have told you that you were crazy."

With the decision to run the business full-time, Ge aimed even higher, making sure he stood out from the pack of custom suit–makers in Chicago. For Ge that meant offering clients truly bespoke, hand-made clothes. "Most 'custom' suits are actually machine-made using

Asian fabrics," he explains about the big brands that use computer imaging scanners. He claims that the products don't live up to the hype. "It's basically airport scanner technology that is repurposed. Unless you are model sized, it doesn't work," he explains. "We are the opposite. While the world goes more digital, we are going to do it analog. We're going to do it the classical way, the right way."

Ge devoted himself to learning everything about the craft of making high-end men's clothes. He did apprenticeships with a variety of tailors to learn about the art of measuring. Today his appointments last an hour, versus the standard ten to twenty minutes, and he takes thirty-four measurements, while most made-to-measure tailors focus on twelve to eighteen spots.

He has visited more than 230 factories and tailors and high-end fabric mills around the world to understand how to make the best suit. "I really didn't understand the difference in fabric—what is good, better, best, or how one fabric versus another is going to work with different body types," he admits.

Ge's business is 75 percent from word of mouth. While corporate types and wedding parties do make up a big part of his business, he has garnered a lot of attention thanks to a steady clientele of Chicago's top athletes and performers who share pictures of their threads on social media. Chance the Rapper, the members of Fall Out Boy, and the football stars Marcus Mariota and Mitch Trubisky all own ESQ originals.

Ge believes that noticing what's missing in the market and figuring out how to provide it is the best way to launch a business. However, he notes that being an entrepreneur isn't something that can really be taught. "You have to be a little crazy," Ge admits. "You just have to believe in your idea, jump off a cliff, and do it."

DON'T FOLLOW
YOUR PASSION

*Having worked countless jobs in her early twenties,
founded a real estate empire with $1,000, and earned TV fame as
one of the entrepreneur investors on* Shark Tank, *Barbara Corcoran
knows all about launching a brand, running a successful business,
mentoring entrepreneurs, and leaping between careers. From how to
negotiate a deal and play to your strengths to not taking no for an
answer, Barbara shares her top pieces of business advice.*

1

TRY A LOT OF DIFFERENT JOBS

You will discover who you are, which of your personality traits are assets, and what gets in your way. I had over twenty jobs before I was 23, and what I quickly found out was the more I could talk with people and be on my feet, the better I was. The less I had to do with writing or reading, the happier I was. Those are great things to learn about yourself, and I wouldn't have discovered them if I'd stayed in only one job.

2

WORKING JUST FROM YOUR HEART DOESN'T ALWAYS WORK

You don't know what your passion is until you walk into it, and that's the truth. People think they have to decide early and they have to get committed to a path. I think that's the worst advice for a young person. In college, I delivered a bouquet of flowers to the same customers every week. That was my passion—I adored flowers. It turned out to be a terrible business for me. I was alone all day going to the flower district, I was alone in the basement packaging up the flowers, and I was alone delivering the flowers to empty doors. The problem was that my great skill is getting along with people. I was so terribly lonely all day long, and I couldn't collaborate with anyone. So it wasn't a good fit.

3

GO WITH YOUR STRENGTHS

Make a list of every job you ever had, even if it was babysitting at age 11. Anything you ever did, paid and unpaid. Write what you liked best and least about each one. You'll see what traits appear and reappear. It is very telling and helpful in terms of what direction you should take.

4

DON'T BE ABOVE ANYTHING

My son is 24, and recently his best friend got fired from a job. Very capable kid, just not the right fit. The first thing my son told him was, "Get a job doing anything." He was right; I second that. You're more hirable when you are working, and your head is in a better place. I landed this kid three restaurant jobs so that he could interview during the day and wait tables at night. He didn't even go for the interviews. I couldn't believe it! If he's a great waiter, he could meet his next employer and go into a career he didn't even know he was going to be good at. I learned more from waitressing than any other job in the world. My career was built on sales, of course, and waitressing done right is a sales/service position.

5

LEARN TO WORK WITH DIFFICULT BOSSES

I never really liked any boss I worked for. But, of course, I had to learn how to get along with all of them. I think what bugged me was a lot of them didn't deserve my respect by the way they ran their operation or treated their employees, but I had to pretend I respected them anyway. Having the wrong boss for a long time can be very damaging to your ego, and it can make you feel less important and less respectful of yourself. So it's important to seek out a situation where you respect yourself for the effort you're making, and chalk up to experience that you've learned to be tolerant.

6

CULTIVATE RISK

I've worked with kids who are super bright, and went to the best schools, and know business. They always have ideas for businesses, but they take consulting jobs instead of making their ideas a reality. They are afraid of the risk. That's what gets in the way, over and over again. I think that being comfortable with risk is essential for anybody starting a business.

7

SURROUND YOURSELF WITH THE RIGHT PEOPLE

That means wildly enthusiastic people who have talent and room to grow. Avoid the clunkers who suck you down—the negative people, the low-energy people, the people who see something wrong with everything, the people who don't aspire. No matter how strong you are, you catch what is near you. I make sure I always have the right atmosphere around me. I learned that years ago.

8

PARTNER WITH SOMEONE WITH THE OPPOSITE STRENGTHS

The most profitable business that I've invested in on *Shark Tank* is Grace & Lace, which is a fashion brand. Why? The same reason all of my good companies are successful: the two entrepreneurs who run it are phenomenal at what they do. One is a designer, one is a business manager: a husband-and-wife team. They have opposite skill sets. It's hard to be good at everything.

9

DON'T TAKE NO FOR AN ANSWER

I signed a contract to do *Shark Tank*, and the producer came back and said they'd changed their mind. So I wrote them an email about why they should hire me. Why did I do that? I'm really good at coming back swinging. Also, I had visualized myself on *Shark Tank*, just like I visualized myself succeeding in New York real estate. Once I've imagined something and work toward that image, it's always come true. If you can't visualize it, you can't get there. For me, that picture is a map of how to get there. It didn't compute for me that it wasn't going to come true. I already had my outfits picked out, I had a pen to sign autographs. I had to come back and fight for it. All it took was a well-written, poignant email.

BUILD A
LEGACY

MONIQUE GREENWOOD

FROM ▶ **TO**

MAGAZINE
EDITOR IN CHIEF

INNKEEPER

SETTING BIG CAREER GOALS I wanted to become editor in chief of *Essence* magazine since high school. To come to work every day and look at the faces of people who looked like me and conceive stories that would inspire people, especially black women, to live their best lives: what an opportunity, what an incredible mission.

DISCOVERING A DIFFERENT LIFESTYLE For three summers, my husband, Glenn Pogue, and I spent a weekend at a bed-and-breakfast in Cape May, New Jersey. The innkeepers seemed to be having an amazing life. The more I spoke to them, the more I realized that owning an inn might not necessarily tie into my professional ambitions but would certainly fit my personal passions. I love meeting people and turning strangers into friends. I love decorating, real estate, and old homes. I was a girl who grew up in a three-bedroom house with seven people and never slept in a room by myself. It was a way to envision how it would be possible to live a lifestyle that I wasn't born into.

FINDING THE PERFECT LOCATION TWO BLOCKS FROM HOME I kept the B&B idea in the back of my mind. One day I was driving in my neighborhood in Brooklyn, and I saw a beautiful wedding. People were spilling out onto the lawn looking fabulous. I saw all this beauty going on, and then I saw all their galvanized trash cans lined up on the street in front of the house. I jumped out and moved the trash cans so they wouldn't ruin the pictures. On my way back to my car I saw the mansion. Even though I had passed it many times before, this time I saw it for what it could be: an amazing B&B.

TURNING A DREAM INTO A REALITY Nobody was living in the mansion, but there was furniture piled up inside. I started leaving notes under the front door, hoping someone would call me back. After two years, I saw a gentleman who told me it was his family home and that there had been a fire. Though the house had suffered, all of the original detail was intact. There were intricately carved marble fireplaces, high ceilings, and beautiful moldings. I was at the Realtor's office the next morning. It turned out, the gentleman owned the house with his siblings, one of them living, and the grandchildren had also become heirs to the estate. It was a yearlong process for the lawyers to get all of their permissions before we could complete the sale.

STUDYING UP ON A NEW CAREER The first thing I did was stay in B&Bs everywhere. I took notes on what I loved and other things that I thought, *When I do mine, I'm not going to do it quite that way.* I took a workshop on running a B&B. I joined the professional trade association for innkeepers to get acquainted with that community. I wanted to have people around me who were doing it and doing it well. I also did a program for entrepreneurs through the Clinton Foundation and one through Goldman Sachs called 10,000 Small Businesses. I signed up for everything to learn all that I needed to know.

APPRECIATING THE FINANCIAL BOOST From a business perspective, I considered myself successful from the day I opened the doors of Akwaaba Mansion in 1995. It was my home, and I had to pay the mortgage and the utilities anyway. That guests could come and share my life but also share my expenses was a double "wow." I didn't have any additional overhead, so it was immediately profitable.

LEAVING *ESSENCE* For six years, I was running Akwaaba Mansion while I was running *Essence* magazine. I had tenants, a business, responsibilities as a wife and mother. I had a desire and responsibility to be a good member of the community. I always had this extremely long list of things to take care of, and I personally never showed up on that list. I realized something had to give, and I quit the magazine.

CREATING A FAMILY LEGACY I'm about legacy building. Although my daughter was 10 at the time, I knew I couldn't leave her my job at *Essence*, but I could leave her a portfolio of real estate and a small family-owned business should she choose to run it.

BUILDING AN EMPIRE Glenn and I had a vision for several more inns. We envisioned that in retirement—which we always planned to do by age 50—we could live in New York in the fall, DC in the spring, and Cape May in the summer. We also liked the idea of New Orleans. The goal was to have four B&Bs—one in each city for each season. Starting in 2002, we opened an inn every two years.

TAKING ON THE CHALLENGE OF MOTHER NATURE We purchased a B&B in New Orleans one month before Hurricane Katrina. We did the best we could trying to keep the inn in business with no income. It was a tremendous financial drain on the other properties. We ended up selling the property, but it took five years.

GOING ON REALITY TV We moved forward with starring in *Checked Inn* on the OWN network, with the intention of shining the light on who we are, how we run the business, and our guests. Oprah saw us as a modern-day Fantasy Island. She knew that we would do everything possible to ensure that the guests staying would have a one-of-a-kind, memorable experience and inspire them to live their best life. From a business perspective, it was like a one-hour commercial for us. The phone rang more than ever.

WORKING LONGER THAN PLANNED When we started, we had the idea that we could retire at 50 and be in a different property every season. The reality is, I'm typically in three states every week. I'm nowhere near retirement. I work harder than ever before, but it is work that fulfills me and drives me.

LOVING WORK THAT DOESN'T FEEL LIKE A JOB I feel I am doing my life's work. I love when my guests have had an experience that exceeds their expectation and I like the change of atmosphere from city life in Brooklyn and DC to small-town living in the Pocono mountains and on the Jersey Shore where we have our inns. Mostly I'm proud I've created something in my own vision that people appreciate and that hopefully I will pass down to my daughter.

CREATE SOMETHING NEW

*Twenty-five years after she started her first company,
Bobbi Brown Cosmetics, 2018 found Bobbi Brown back in major-launch
mode. She started a lifestyle website, JustBobbi, a new health
and beauty brand, Evolution_18, and she opened a hotel in Montclair,
New Jersey, the George. On top of all that, she's back in school studying
nutrition. The makeup artist turned mogul shares her experience and
advice for would-be entrepreneurs.*

1
LOOK FOR A GAP IN THE MARKET

When I started my brand, I had no clue what I was doing. I did not go to business school. I just knew that I couldn't find makeup that looked natural, so I went for it. I teamed up with a chemist to make ten lipsticks in natural shades. It disrupted the market, which in the 1990s was all about over-the-top colors. My makeup was different. That's the key; you need to create something new.

2
MAKE SURE YOU ARE BETTER THAN THE COMPETITION

Whatever you are making needs to stand out from what's already out there. Copying other products isn't a business plan. How many people can put shea butter in a jar and call it a business? Think about why people would buy your product over what's out there. If there's a solid reason to try yours, then you're on to something.

3

SAVE MONEY

Invest in your business, but cut out everything else that's not essential to what you are building. Live with relatives or friends to save on rent. Keep your day job, and work nights and weekends until your new gig takes off.

4

ASK FRIENDS TO HELP

When you have an exciting new idea, people want to help and be involved. Let them. When I started Bobbi Brown Cosmetics, my husband used to mail lipsticks, and my sister-in-law helped with accounting. If you don't have the money to hire a lawyer, ask a friend with legal training to help you with contracts and negotiations. Calling in a few favors at first can really pay off.

5

TEST YOUR PRODUCT

When I was creating my lipsticks, I had my friends try them out. They let me know what they liked and what they didn't. Their input was crucial to making the product better. You don't need to pay money for an official focus group like the big brands do. Find your target market, and let them sample the product in exchange for a mention on social media or honest feedback.

6

CREATE A LOOK THAT'S ALL YOUR OWN

A signature visual style and cool packaging is as important as the actual product. It's the first thing people see, and people make judgments. You don't need fancy, expensive packaging—you just want something that stands out. Sometimes simple is best. Take a look at all the cool indie brands out there for #inspo.

7

BE STRONG ON SOCIAL

You need organic growth to launch a brand. That happens through word of mouth, whether that is people telling their friends in person or on social. I think Instagram is the single greatest tool to grow a business. It is all about visual branding. The hashtags help you target your audience. The comments act as feedback to make your brand stronger. It acts as marketing and PR. Most important, it is free.

8

CALM DOWN

A lot of people are frantic when they start a new business. They think they have to be an overnight success. You need to slow down, hit the pause button every once in a while. Take a day to ask yourself, *What's working? What isn't? What else can I do?*

KNOW WHEN TO TRY
SOMETHING NEW

You're going to have a lot of obstacles, so prepare for those. But after a certain amount of time, if everything is going wrong, you're not making money, you're not getting good feedback, people aren't offering to help, you're not able to produce what you had in mind: step back. It could just be timing, but it may be a sign to pivot your idea or go for something new. Just because one idea doesn't work doesn't mean the next one won't.

3

CHOOSE
YOUR OWN
ADVENTURE

—

Live on a Boat / Downward Dog Around the Globe /
Make the Ocean Your Office /
Get Paid to Travel / See the World

EVERYONE HAS THAT THOUGHT while on vacation. That moment of *Why am I going back to my stressed-out life?*

On your trip, you will meet a handful of people who seem wildly happy with their full-time life in vacationland. In casual conversation, they will ask you: "Where do you live? What do you do?" You will answer. Whether it is a city or a suburb, a desk job or one where you're on your feet all day, they will shake their heads and say, "Man, I used to live that life. It just wasn't for me."

That's when you begin to wonder, *Why don't I stay here forever?*

This chapter features a brave group who chose to live a life of adventure, setting sail, diving underwater, leading safaris, moving to a new country every three months, and exploring new destinations. They get paid to travel. They've found a way to live and work abroad.

They will tell you that moving around the world and leaving behind friends and family and a life you've known forever isn't always easy. There are hurdles such as homesickness, bureaucracy, language, and cultural barriers. But the folks in this chapter have discovered strengths they didn't know they had, become part of local communities, and tapped into a new version of themselves.

That moment on vacation where they thought, *I'm staying!* They made it happen.

Where will you land?

LIVE ON THE
WATER

BRITTANY & SCOTT MEYERS

FROM

RECRUITING AND
SALES PEOPLE

TO

OWNERS OF A
CHARTER SAILBOAT
COMPANY

"Living on a self-sufficient off-grid sailboat is significantly cheaper than living in the suburbs..."

BRITTANY AND SCOTT MEYERS both grew up sailing in Michigan, but they didn't meet until they moved to Chicago after college. Brittany took a job as a recruiting manager for a start-up and Scott was in merchandise sales for athletes. They met while racing against each other on Lake Michigan. "Sailing quickly became central to our union," explains Brittany. Now they are the owners of Aristocat Charters in

Tortola. Here's how they created their dream life and have weathered the storms that come with living in paradise.

When did you get the idea you wanted to "live a life less ordinary"?

BRITTANY: I am not entirely sure where the idea to stray from the normal path came from, but after college I moved to Tanzania, where I lived for three years. It was one of the most profound, life-changing, and incredible periods. After that experience, I was ruined for the American Dream. The standard track of living in the suburbs and working in an office might work for a lot of people, but it never seemed appealing to me. I like to think of my life like a book. I want it not only to be a great story but to have interesting settings, characters, and plot twists.

How did you finance those first two years sailing in the Caribbean?

BRITTANY: We left Chicago with a nice chunk of savings from our jobs. We bought a Hallberg-Rassy Rasmus 35 cruising boat and sailed down to Grenada, because Scott got a job at Island Windjammers, where he was a relief captain working six weeks on, two months off. Living on a self-sufficient off-grid sailboat is significantly cheaper than living in the suburbs, so his salary more than covered our lifestyle.

What did you love most about sailing as a couple? What were the challenges?

SCOTT: The freedom! We could go wherever we wanted, whenever we wanted, with only the weather limiting us. We also enjoyed not knowing what lay ahead each day. We were constantly discovering cool things to do and explore. As for what the challenges were, I think it goes without saying there are numerous issues that can arise when you live with your spouse in a space smaller than most people's bedrooms.

How did things change when you started cruising with your first daughter, Isla?

BRITTANY: We enjoyed cruising even more. We went from island to island, spending most nights at anchor. The toughest part of cruising with a baby was when it got rough. Scott would be trying to handle the boat all by himself, and I'd just be holding her below deck to keep her safe. Luckily, those days were very rare, as we are sticklers about watching weather. Our life followed her schedule, which was limiting, but it worked.

SCOTT: We upgraded to a Brewer 44 after she was born, so we had a bit more space. Isla became a little ambassador in a sense and opened doors to meet people we might otherwise not have met. People tended to be a bit warmer and more inviting to our family.

How did you adjust when you had your twins?

BRITTANY: When we discovered that I was pregnant with twins, I freaked out. I had no idea how we'd make it work on a boat with three kids under three. But I was determined to give them the same kind of magical babyhood we gave Isla. We decided we'd bring the twins aboard at 10 months old and settle in the British Virgin Islands. We bought a charter company, Aristocat Charters, and that became our livelihood. We knew we could still enjoy the elements of cruising that we loved—beautiful sailing, short passages, nights at anchor, a multi-cultural community, and lots of time in nature—without the things we didn't like, namely, long passages and rough weather.

What's your life in Tortola like?

BRITTANY: Our kids run amok barefoot, and we feel free to parent without helicoptering. It's a very safe and small community. Our kids are outside most of their waking hours, using their imaginations, playing in the sand, climbing trees, swimming in the ocean. It's a bit simpler down here, and we love it. Our kids are virtually screen free, and life is like it was thirty years ago in many ways.

What is it like making your home in the British Virgin Islands as Americans?

SCOTT: Vacationing on an island and living on an island are two very different things. It's not easy, especially trying to run our day sail business, and everything requires a lot of patience. Things run at a much slower pace here, which can be frustrating. We are constantly having to renew permits, wait in lines, and we need permission to stay here every year. As non-islander business owners, hiring people is very hard and can easily take four to six months.

You were living a dream life, and then the 2017 hurricanes hit. How did they impact your life and business?

BRITTANY: They really turned our life upside down. We were on track to pay off our business and had plans to start traveling again. We had just hired an operations manager to take some of the workload off Scott's plate, as he was working eighteen-hour days regularly. Irma changed everything. Not only did she sink our home and almost all of our worldly possessions, she destroyed our business boats, while simultaneously seriously crippling tourism, the one thing we need for our business to survive. We have way too much invested in this place to give up. Thankfully, we had insurance. We purchased a new day charter boat, and we are back up and running, albeit in a much lower capacity than before. It will take a good long while to get back to where we were. All the things we love about the island are still here. We will not be here forever. The world is too big. But for now this is home.

LIVE ON A BOAT

*Does sailing in the Caribbean sound like the life for you?
The co-owner of Aristocat Charters, Brittany Meyers, shares five steps
to swapping life on land for one at sea.*

LEARN TO SAIL

Getting involved in your local sailing club is the cheapest and most comprehensive way to learn. There are also many pay-to-sail organizations where you can get a position on a boat for a week as a trainee. However, the learning curve will be steep.

TEST OUT LIVING ON BOARD

Sailing a boat and living on one are two very different things. Take a sailing vacation where you rent a boat and stay aboard for a week. If you are comfortable captaining by yourself, get on a bareboat charter, or if you'd rather someone else helm the ship, join a crewed charter.

DOWNSIZE

The average boat is much smaller than most homes. Paring down to the bare essentials is actually quite liberating. Minimalism is key to life on a boat. A good rule of thumb: if it doesn't serve two purposes, it doesn't come aboard.

DECIDE WHICH BOAT IS RIGHT FOR YOU

Determining what sort of boat you want is a big decision. How big of a boat do you need? Do you want a fixer-upper or something newer? Do you plan to cross oceans or simply island-hop? I suggest the book *How Not to Buy a Cruising Boat* to help you decide.

MOVE ABOARD

Before you sail off to far-flung places, live on the boat for a good amount of time. Boats are intricate and have many systems; more often than not, you will be the one having to fix and maintain them. Learn your boat, take small practice cruises, and get ready to set sail.

DEFY
EXPECTATIONS

FROM

REAL ESTATE
LAWYER

TO

SURF CAMP
FOUNDER

> *"I don't know that I had natural talent, but I had dedication, perseverance, and persistence."*

GROWING UP IN TEXAS, Ashley Blaylock was inseparable from her older brother, Josh. But when he started skateboarding and surfing, she held back. "I think I subconsciously thought, *Oh, he's a guy, he can do that, but I can't,*" says Ashley. It wasn't until college that she realized that her perception of surfing as a sport just for guys was way off base. "One of my best friends was really into surfing and it was the first time I thought, *Wait—if she can do this, then I can, too.*" It took only one outing to Surfside, a beach an hour from Houston, for an entirely new world to open up. "I was hooked right away."

Although Ashley loved her time on the water, the sport didn't come easily. "Surfing is extremely challenging and incredibly physically demanding. I spent the first year floundering around," she admits. "I don't know that I had natural talent, but I had dedication, perseverance, and persistence."

Throughout college and law school, Ashley surfed every chance she could. Hoping to get closer to better breaks, she even signed up for a law school semester abroad in Costa Rica. On a side trip, she discovered the surfing mecca San Juan del Sur in Nicaragua, which boasted a friendly community, killer waves, and an unspoiled backdrop.

In Nicaragua, Ashley immediately stood out. "There were no female surfers in San Juan and not many Americans," she recalls. The guides from the surf shop were in disbelief when she joined their day trip. "They were like, 'Wait, you're going out on the waves? You can't surf! We've never seen a girl surf.'" Ashley loved proving them wrong. "I wasn't a good surfer, but I had the balls to go for the big waves. They were like, 'Wow! Chica brava!' which means 'brave girl.'"

It didn't take long for Ashley to fall in love with Nicaragua. "Within forty-eight hours I thought, *Man, I want to live here.*" The visit also gave her insight into a career she didn't know existed. "The surf guides seemed like they were living the dream. I thought, *I would love to do this.*" Ashley imagined herself teaching other women how to ride the waves fearlessly, but she also thought it would never happen. "I was in law school. I had been studying my whole life to be a lawyer, and I knew I was going to have tens of thousands of dollars in debt when I was done."

Still, Ashley returned to San Juan del Sur every vacation she had from law school. During those two years, the town grew exponentially and the real estate market boomed. The idea of living there persisted. Graduating in the top quarter of her class with a specialty in tax and corporate law, Ashley had plenty of opportunities in Houston, but by then she also had contacts in Nicaragua. When she heard of an opening at a Nicaraguan law firm doing real estate transactions, she leapt at the chance and moved to San Juan del Sur. A few months later, Coldwell Banker hired her to be its in-house transaction coordinator in Nicaragua.

> "
> *It was*
> EMPOWERING
> *to have people*
> *doubt my abilities*
> *and show them how*
> POWERFUL
> *women can be.*

For a lot of people, the story would have ended there: finding a way to practice law in paradise. However, Ashley also wanted to take her surfing to the next level. She tried to convince organizers of local surf competitions to let her enter and compete against the guys, but they didn't go for it. Instead, she persuaded them to add a women's category. That year, she became the female surf champion of Nicaragua—a title she held on to for six years.

Even though Ashley was building a lucrative career as a lawyer, she found herself wanting to be out of the office and on the water all the time. "I was living a life that sounds amazing on paper, but I had another dream—to open a surf camp for women—but I wasn't doing anything to make it a reality," she says. "Then my grandmother died, and it brought everything into sharp focus. Life is short. So I took my idea off the back burner."

Ashley's initial reluctance to try surfing as a teen and the expectations she'd had to defy as a female surfer in Nicaragua fueled her business idea. "It was empowering to have people doubt my abilities and show them how powerful women can be." She named her surf school Chica Brava.

Ashley initially kept her day job and invested only $500 to launch a website and a few hundred more for PR. To save money she did everything else herself, even picking up clients from the airport. Despite warnings from friends that she wouldn't make any money, the business was successful enough in its first year for her to focus on it full-time.

In addition to hosting women from around the world looking to ride the waves, Ashley began partnering with a local school to do monthly outreach work with teen girls. "Our main mission is empowerment and to break the mold of gender inequality that they are growing up in. We want them to think about roles and careers they haven't thought of," she says. "We tell them, 'When you get the reaction from people that you can't do something, know that you actually can.'"

Ashley feels that she is teaching so much more than surf skills. "You can never really master it. You can't control the ocean. It is so physically demanding. It can be frustrating, but when you overcome the hurdles, it becomes a metaphor for life," she reflects. "Surfing teaches you to be fierce because you face your fears head-on."

GET OUT OF YOUR
COMFORT
ZONE

ALLISON FLEECE & DANIELLE THORNTON

FROM  **TO**

INTERNATIONAL
EDUCATION AND
ADVERTISING
EXECUTIVES

FOUNDERS OF A
PHILANTHROPIC
WOMEN'S
ADVENTURE TRAVEL
COMPANY

*"When you find something that lights you on fire,
you have to just do it."*

IT TOOK ONLY A glimpse of Mount Kilimanjaro for Allison Fleece to know she had to climb it. The sighting, on the way to the airport after a safari trip to Tanzania, made this nonclimber suddenly want to scale peaks. "I thought it was probably the most beautiful thing I had seen with my own two eyes," she explains. "I vowed I would come back. Maybe it was to prove to myself what I was capable of achieving mentally and physically, but I couldn't stop thinking about it."

When Allison got back to New York, where she worked advising students on international educational opportunities, she sent out an email to the most adventurous people she could think of. The subject line read "I'm going to climb Kili. Who's in?" A mutual friend forwarded it to Danielle Thornton, then working as a creative director at an advertising agency in New York. Despite the fact that she, too, had never climbed a mountain, Danielle liked the idea of a challenging experience that would break up the grind of her job. Before she even had time to really think about what she was signing up for, she agreed to go.

Allison and Danielle planned the trip for the following year with a total of ten women. To prep, they did multiple training hikes in upstate New York with their boots and backpacks to get used to trekking with the same equipment they would use for the thirty-five-mile climb on Kilimanjaro.

The experience of climbing Kilimanjaro was life-changing. "To be able to realize that your body and mind can set your sights on something so big and enormous as climbing one of the seven summits— and actually accomplish it—is an incredible feeling," explains Allison. "There is also something powerful about the bond that happens when you experience the climb with other people. You have to really support each other."

Even though the trek was mentally and physically grueling, it also felt exhilarating. "We both got really sick early on. It was twice as hard, because we were both fighting our own bodies to get to the top. As hard as it was, we did it," recalls Danielle. "As soon as we got down, we looked at each other and said, 'How can we do this again?'"

Committed to making travel their job, Allison and Danielle started hatching a business plan on the plane ride home. "The trip gave me a new, broader perspective of the world and lit something up within me. I was so changed and moved, I didn't want to go back to the life I was living before," says Danielle. "The month prior, I had one of my ads run in the Super Bowl, but I just didn't care anymore. At the end of the day, I was selling light beer."

Allison and Danielle quickly came up with the idea of leading other women on similarly transformative trips. More than just travel, they wanted to include a way to give back and bond with local women as part of their business plan for Women High on Adventure or WHOA Travel. "So often in travel, we take, but we wanted to approach this adventure from a sharing perspective," explains Allison. "We believe experiences are more meaningful when you connect with the local community."

On that first trip, their climbing group raised $5,000 for a women's vocational school at the base of Kilimanjaro. "The Tanzanians shared their mountain with us, and we wanted to share in return." At the end of their climb, they spent a day at the school getting to know the students. "The women had lots of questions about what climbing Kilimanjaro was like," says Danielle. "They grew up seeing it every day and knew it was a huge part of the economy in the region, but few locals, especially women, have the opportunity to climb it unless they are guides."

Now WHOA Travel invites local women to do the climbs as part of the group. "It allows our travelers to get to know women from the region they are visiting," says Danielle. "But it also inspires men, children, and whole communities. They see women from their village taking on something that traditionally is held as a man's space, and everyone walks away from the experience with a more empowered perspective."

The first year of WHOA Travel, Danielle and Allison planned trips to Tanzania (Kilimanjaro climb), Peru (Salkantay to Machu Picchu trek), and Bavaria (Oktoberfest), finding nonprofit partners in each country. Their first trip to Oktoberfest had only three clients, all of whom had learned about the trip through word of mouth. Five months later, their trip to Kilimanjaro on International Women's Day had thirty women. "I think that's when we knew we were on to something and that this was absolutely something women wanted in their lives," says Allison. Now WHOA Travel goes to Kilimanjaro and Peru multiple times a year, and has added India, Iceland, Mount Elbrus in the Caucasus Mountains of southern Russia, and Everest Base Camp to its lineup.

Allison and Danielle say they have been able to make WHOA Travel work partly because their business model doesn't involve a lot of up-front capital, requires no office space, and has a work flow that can be managed by a core team that can work remotely. They were able to launch with no outside investors, relying on savings and freelance work for the first two years to supplement trip sale income. "My salary is now comparable to what I was making in advertising," says Danielle. "But my quality of life and the hours I am working are so much better that it isn't possible to make a comparison. We are getting paid to travel the world with a rock star group of women." Adds Allison, "When you find something that lights you on fire, you have to just do it."

DOWNWARD DOG AROUND THE GLOBE

MARINA DE LIMA

FROM ▸ **TO**

REALITY TV PRODUCER ▸ NOMADIC YOGA INSTRUCTOR

I WAS A REALITY TV PRODUCER in New York for over a decade. Everyone in TV is constantly stressed, but it gave me a rush and a thrill and a purpose. Plus, I was good at talking to people and getting them to open up and share their stories on camera.

After about six years, I noticed the things that I loved so much had started to lose their luster. I felt the toll the job was taking. I would feel this emotional high if a show did well and the worst low if it didn't. I wondered what I was actually doing. I thought, *Why am I looking to exploit people? It's not making me better or them better.* I was becoming kind of angry and mean.

I moved into a new apartment, and I remember looking around

thinking I had everything I wanted: the boyfriend, the job with the high salary, the expensive bag and shoes, and a big social life. But still I felt like there was something missing.

I took a yoga class and immediately noticed a difference in how I felt. My friends thought it was funny. "Marina, *you* are doing yoga?" They saw me as super intense. They thought it was a fad like when I lifted weights or started sewing. But I understood immediately that yoga was fulfilling what I was missing. I thought, *This is making me better. I am becoming whole.*

After three years, a teacher mentioned that she was running a teacher training program and thought I'd enjoy it. I told her I had a very demanding job and no desire to teach yoga. She offered me the training for free in return for some promotional filming for her. It was very serendipitous that she saw something in me that I had yet to see.

After I completed my two-hundred-hour fundamental training, I went to India to pursue advanced training and took a hard look at my life. *What kind of woman am I becoming?* I wasn't happy with what I saw. I had this catalog of failed relationships. I had no intimacy with anyone. My work was unfulfilling. I knew something had to change, but I still wasn't quite sure how. When I got back to New York, I took a job on a show that let me travel, but it wasn't enough.

A friend introduced me to Jorge Branco via email, thinking we would have a lot in common. He was starting a business organizing volunteer retreats. We talked on the phone about both wanting to live a different kind of life, but the difference was, he was doing it and I wasn't. Jorge was starting a business doing ten-day adventure trips that included a volunteer project.

We spent four days together, and Jorge told me he wanted to include yoga on his trips and offered me the opportunity to join him in Morocco. I knew I had to go. I needed to commit and break up with this life already. It was now or never.

My family couldn't understand what I was doing. People dream of the life I was living in New York, but the dream didn't work for me anymore. It was my whole family's dream that I had to say good-bye to. I was crying as I packed up my apartment, almost mourning my old life, but I knew I had to do it.

Jorge and I lived in Morocco together, and then I went back to India and spent time in Nepal and Bali before joining him in a very remote village in Nicaragua. Through our nonprofit, World Travelers Association, we've run retreats in Ecuador, Portugal, Malaysia, Nicaragua, Cambodia, Bali, Iceland, and India. We combine yoga, adventure, and service into singular trips. He and I are partners now in business and in life.

In TV I was making $3,000 a week. As a yoga instructor, I have had to figure out how to make $1,000 stretch for three months. In the beginning, I was still trying to live my old life, so I went through my savings in the first few months. I was conditioned for so many years to live a certain way—getting my nails done, ordering food, getting my eyebrows waxed. When I was in Nicaragua, where the living conditions are really rough—no electricity, no hot water or some days no water at all—I realized I was a little bit of a princess!

Thailand was the first country where we were able to make some money, and we have been steadily increasing our earnings and thinking of additional ways to bring in income, such as doing yoga

> **"**
> *People dream of the life I was living in New York, but the dream didn't work for me anymore.*

teacher trainings. In 2017, I made about $22,000, which was almost double my living allotment of the previous year. Living simply and in third-world countries, that amount of money can stretch very far.

I chose an alternative lifestyle that would bring me rewards that were greater than monetary gain. But rewards such as experiences, memories, self-expansion, inner peace, and love can seem so trivial when I still have to make money, run a business, and deal with external factors that may not be rooted in the same intentions as mine.

The hardest thing is learning to adapt to all the change. I just need to remember that I chose this. I chose to leave my family and friends and roam around the world, moving every couple of months so I can have the joy of beginning again somewhere new. Saying good-bye is part of the story.

There will never be the right time or the perfect opportunity. You will never have the right amount of money saved to do this. Had I waited and not jumped on the opportunity as it was presented to me, I probably would've chickened out and never left. Although it was scary, I needed to plunge deeply into the life I wanted and seize the chance I was given.

MAKE THE
OCEAN
YOUR OFFICE

NADIA ALY

FROM

SOCIAL
MEDIA
MARKETER

TO

FOUNDER OF A
SCUBA WEBSITE,
UNDERWATER
PHOTOGRAPHER

> *"I don't like the idea of a nine-to-five job. I find it very boring and repetitive, and getting only two weeks off each year is crazy."*

DIVING IN I grew up in Canada. My parents don't swim. When we would go on vacation, other family friends would take me snorkeling. I loved being in the water. I got my first certification for scuba diving when I was 13.

BECOMING OBSESSED WITH SCUBA DIVING My first job was in social media marketing at Microsoft. While I was there, I entered a video to an online contest and ended up winning a scuba-diving trip through Tourism Fiji. The trip ignited this passion for scuba diving. When I got back, I tried to look up everything I could: where to see whale sharks, where to see hammerheads. The websites I found in 2010 looked like they had been built in the late 1990s. I couldn't learn anything from them. Scuba diving is such an offline industry, run by an older generation of people who don't understand digital media and diving. So I started ScubaDiverLife.com to create a modern digital community.

GROWING THE WEBSITE I was doing the site on the side, but I knew that I needed original content to grow. So I bought the best underwater photo and video equipment I could afford, but before I left the store I realized I didn't even know how to use it all. The shop's owners were hosting an underwater photography trip to Bonaire, and I signed up. For five days all my photos were black, but then I got it.

GETTING A WAKE-UP CALL A year later, I visited Google for my work and thought, *This is where I want to be! At the forefront of technology.* I landed an interview, but during the process, I found out my best friend's brother Dave had died, four hours before his twenty-eighth birthday. It really shook me up. I ended up getting the job, but I left after eight months. Dave's death changed everything for me. I became awake to what I didn't want in life. While I was at Google, I kept thinking, *Is this going to be my life? I don't want this to be my life.* The yearning to scuba dive around the world kept growing.

TRYING TO MERGE TECH AND ADVENTURE After leaving Google, I ended up doing marketing for an association called PADI (Professional Association of Diving Instructors). It is the number one association for scuba-diving certification in the world. At first it seemed like a perfect fit, but I wasn't in the ocean. I wasn't on trips. I wasn't hanging out with hammerheads. I was still behind a desk.

FACING DOWN FEAR I started ScubaDiverLife.com as a hobby, but by the time I was at PADI it had 300,000 fans and had become a platform. I decided to try to turn it into something bigger, and I quit my job. I felt lost when I left PADI, but I knew I wanted to dive the world and grow my site. I think fear really held me back from doing it earlier. I was born and raised in Canada, where health care is taken care of. In the United States it costs over $14,000 a year to have medical insurance.

GROWING THE BRAND Because I was in marketing, I knew exactly how to grow the Facebook community with ads and original content. Within a month I had steady advertising income from diving companies and tourism boards. I had an advantage because there were no other online scuba-diving sites. In the beginning, I was making $3,000 or $4,000 a month just from ads.

DIVING AROUND THE WORLD To make content, I needed to get on the road. I was able to exchange reviews and content creation to go on trips with dive operators. All I had to pay for was my suit and flight. I've been able to work with several tourism boards—including the Cayman Islands, Dominica, Bali, and Bermuda—to show people why they are diving destinations. That pretty much carried me for two years. In 2014, I hired an editor, so now I just focus on sales and content.

LEADING EXPEDITIONS I was constantly underwater, and I got very good at photography. I had people license my images, and I developed a personal brand online. That led to taking people on trips to teach them how to take photos underwater. This year I have a hammerhead trip to the Bahamas and diving trips to Sudan, South Africa, Indonesia, Antarctica, and the Galapagos.

SEEING OPPORTUNITY This is my third year of running a trip to Tonga. It is pretty easy to sell; it's not diving, just snorkeling, and I am taking people to swim with humpback whales. I bought a house in Tonga to put my clients in. In my vision I could work in Tonga July through October and then take my own trips the rest of the year. I can easily see myself being there for twenty years. When you have your own business you try something and see if it works, and if it does, you go even further with it.

FACING UP TO THE FINANCIAL REALITY In the past five years I've been able to travel almost year-round and buy the gear that I need. However, this is the first year I might potentially make a profit through the site and the expedition company. People ask me all the time how to do what I am doing. The first thing I tell them is, "You aren't going to make money unless you want to own a dive shop or you are the top photographer. If you want to have a family or buy a house, forget about it. Most of the people in the dive industry are in their early twenties, and they are doing it for experience."

WORKING OUTDOORS I don't like the idea of a nine-to-five job. I find it very boring and repetitive, and getting only two weeks off each year is crazy. I don't think that humans should live like that. I'm able to explore the world and the oceans, see new cultures, and meet new people. That's exactly how I want to live.

GO FOR IT
EVEN IF YOU'RE AFRAID

TALLEY SMITH

FROM ▸

TRUST
ADMINISTRATOR

TO ▸

SAFARI RANGER IN
SOUTH AFRICA

THE RULE IN THE BUSH IS: When you come across a wild animal on foot, don't run. If you show an animal that you are confident just by standing there, sometimes it will get confused and think, *Why are they standing there? Should I be afraid?* If you run, you are showing submission, and it may try to take advantage of that and chase you down because it feels like it has the upper hand. It does feel very counterintuitive to stand there as opposed to running away, but that is what you have to do.

This applies to life as well. If something is giving you that feeling of fear (for me, it feels physically like a pit in my stomach) and you don't really want to deal with it, that is a sign that you have to do it. You have to address it. You've got to go for it. Don't run away. If you have that feeling of fear about something, it actually should be pulling you toward it rather than pushing you away. Once you get through it, you feel like a different person. It brings you this new sense of confidence.

I grew up in Bermuda, and I was working in finance in my twenties. I just always had that feeling that there was something more out there for me. I never sat behind my desk and thought, *I want to be a game ranger in Africa*. I never thought that was a possibility for me! I did know, however, that I loved nature and I loved wildlife, and I wanted to go to South Africa to explore it. I booked a vacation, planning on being here for only a few weeks.

On my trip, I saw a leopard in the wild, and I remember being blown away by the experience. Growing up in Bermuda, I hadn't really been a part of that type of wilderness before. It was really quite moving. I remember that moment, thinking to myself, *There is this world out there that is so much bigger than we are*. I knew then that it was something I wanted to continue to be a part of somehow.

I went back to Bermuda for two weeks, and I said to my family, "I love it, I'm going back." They thought I was completely crazy. Obviously, they didn't really understand it. They had never been to southern Africa, they'd just heard the sometimes horrible things that get portrayed on the news with crime and things like that. They just had to trust me.

I came back to Africa with a plan to live off of my savings for a few months while I did volunteer work to gain experience. I started as an intern at a lodge in the Okavango Delta, Botswana, assisting with operational duties. Then I met a female ranger named Jana who told me I should look into becoming a ranger since I was clearly passionate about nature and wildlife.

Being a ranger is being a part of a male-dominated industry.

> "
> *If you have that*
> **FEELING OF FEAR**
> *about something, it*
> *actually should be*
> PULLING YOU
> TOWARD IT
> *rather than pushing*
> *you away.*

The few female rangers that I met were really tough. I really tipped my hat to them, but it wasn't until I met Jana that I felt it was something I could do. She was very gentle, yet she still did the job with her rifle, changing spare tires, leading groups, just as well as anyone else.

To become a guide, especially if you are not from South Africa, you need to do ranger training. That's how a lot of people from overseas break in. It is a lot of driving training, basic knowledge about wildlife, studying ecology, and then the rifle training. The truth is, you get most of your knowledge on the job, particularly when it comes to learning animal behavior.

My training program took about six months. Certain things were challenging for me. In Bermuda, firearms are illegal. I'd never even seen a gun, let alone fired one. I worked hard to master it. The toughest parts are the assessments that test speed and accuracy using a rifle under pressure. When you challenge yourself, you end up surprising yourself a lot of the time.

After training I got a job at a lodge as a junior guide. They really took a chance in hiring me, this blond girl from Bermuda fresh out of guiding school. I worked there for two years, and then I came to Londolozi Game Reserve, which has its own intense training program to test strength and character and how you operate in the wilderness. The whole program is designed to make you push yourself and still have faith in the fact that you are able to take care of your guests in a potentially dangerous situation. One of the things that it requires is that you go out in the bush for a week and fend for yourself. It is incredibly mental and physical walking around for miles and bumping into a rhino, or being eye to eye with a venomous snake, or finding yourself in a huge herd of elephants, then relying on yourself to make the right decision. It's not only a question of *Can I do this to get the job that I want?* but also *Am I going to make it out alive*? I had to push myself until I found these places within myself that I didn't know were there.

I am now head ranger at Londolozi, overseeing twenty-five rangers and twenty-five trackers. I find it quite amusing that I am the boss of all men. When people ask me how I got here, I tell them, "You may not know what the end goal is, and that's okay. You just have to step out of the box you're in and take risks that may seem a little bit crazy at the time."

HOW I GOT HERE

Talley Smith's path to head ranger

BABYSITTER

AQUARIUM INTERN

VENTURE CAPITAL ASSISTANT

HORSE STABLE WORKER

TRUST ADMINISTRATOR

LODGE INTERN

GAME COMPANY INTERN

GAME RESERVE GUIDE

LONDOLOZI GAME RESERVE HEAD RANGER

GET PAID TO
TRAVEL

EULANDA OSAGIEDE

FROM

DANCE TEACHER

TO

COFOUNDER AND CONTENT
CREATOR OF A LIFESTYLE WEBSITE

OMO OSAGIEDE

DAY JOB

RISK MANAGEMENT INFORMATION
TECHNOLOGY MANAGER

SIDE HUSTLE

COFOUNDER AND CONTENT
CREATOR OF A LIFESTYLE WEBSITE

> *"We had been treating this as a passion project.
> What could we do if we put our minds to it?"*

I T WAS A DATING APP that connected Eulanda, a former dance teacher and wedding photographer from Colorado, and Omo, an IT executive from Lagos, Nigeria. Six years ago, they were both living in London, and both put on their profiles that they were passionate about food and travel. The site's algorithm worked its magic and the couple connected, falling in love while traveling, cooking, and exploring their new city.

Eulanda and Omo wanted to document their trips to share with friends and family beyond Facebook, so they started a blog as an online diary of their adventures. "In the beginning it was 'Let's cook something this weekend. Let's write a story. Let's show these pictures.' We weren't thinking about it in a very journalistic fashion," says Omo.

Eulanda was able to channel her skills as a photographer, and the site evolved to feature recipes and destination guides, with musings on health, relationships, and trying new things. They called it Hey! Dip Your Toes In, which is sort of a mantra for the duo, who always aim to get out of their comfort zone to create a rich life for themselves.

Hey! Dip Your Toes In launched in March 2015, and at the end of that year, on a whim, Omo submitted the site for the UK Blog Awards. By spring of 2016, they were finalists in both the food and travel categories. "We thought that in itself was a big achievement," says Omo. They were both shocked and thrilled when they actually won in the Food and Drink category and were runner-up in the Travel category. "That was a wake-up call that we had been treating this as a passion project," says Omo. "What could we do if we put our minds to it?"

Brands, TV producers, and editors started reaching out to them. "The awards didn't make us superstars overnight; our numbers were still low, and we had to grow the network and community organically, but it gave us more credibility to be able to have conversations with brands we weren't able to approach before," explains Omo. After they completed their first brand partnership with IBM a few months later, the duo turned their focus to content creation—essentially making their blog a digital platform where they get paid to publish stories for food and travel brands.

In the early days, they were just documenting their own adventures. Now they're getting paid to travel. "We went on a cruise to see the Grand Prix in Monaco. I went on assignment with *House of Coco* magazine to Abu Dhabi. Etihad flew me out business class, hosted me in the gorgeous Yas Viceroy for six days, and I attended Taste of Abu Dhabi as their VIP guest," says Eulanda. "It has been unbelievable the opportunities we have had."

Omo continues to work in IT, focusing on the blog on the side, while Eulanda eventually left her teaching job to work on the site full-time. "I was in the dance world and the performing arts world and not achieving the level of success I would have preferred," says Eulanda. "Now being able to use so many parts of myself has been a dream come true."

As the site has thrived, so has their relationship. "The opportunity to work together as a couple has tested us. The benefits are amazing: you get to know each other in a whole different way, you learn a lot about patience and give-and-take," says Eulanda. "The important part of this ecosystem is the two of us. We are building a dream for each other."

Eulanda and Omo are quick to admit that although their website has given them countless travel opportunities, it has required a

tremendous amount of work to make it financially viable as a career. There is this fantasy of giving up your career and traveling around the world, sustaining
yourself with a few articles here and
there. However, such a career is a
24/7 operation that requires out-of-
the-box thinking to create lasting
income. "If there is a possibility to
go into content creation, you need to
have a strong plan; it's not for the faint
of heart," says Eulanda. "Have some
savings, don't just walk away from your
job. It is not realistic! There are so few bloggers who have gotten to a point where they are
earning all of their income through blogging. You have
to create multiple streams of income."

INCOME STREAM
YOUR WAY TO SUCCESS

Getting paid to travel requires a lot of work and creative thinking, so Eulanda and Omo target these ten different money-making opportunities. Bloggers, take note.

1
RETREATS

Twice a year, we host destination-based retreats for small businesses and creative entrepreneurs. We travel with bloggers or content creators looking for some coaching. We're set to earn an average of £2,000 [about $2,600] per retreat in 2018.

2
WORKSHOPS

We host three-hour workshops for content creators that are focused on teaching coveted skills within the industry, such as video editing, pitching, and working with brands. In the past, we've earned an average of £300 [about $400] per workshop.

3
CAMPAIGNS

We create custom in-depth content campaigns for travel and food brands. These campaigns feature multiple types of content such as video, infographics, photos, copy, polls, and social media posts. Then we'll run the content campaign for two to three weeks. Our starter package begins at £699 [about $900].

4
FOOD PHOTOGRAPHY AND DESTINATION FILMS

This is currently our most consistent and highest-yielding stream of income. We work with tourism boards, food tour companies, and a range of other clients. We anticipate earning £15,000-plus [about $19,500] this year.

5

COACHING

We offer personalized coaching for entrepreneurs in the creative sector. We have a three-month package that runs £1,500 [about $1,950]. Or clients can ask us anything in virtual coaching calls for £25 [about $30] per fifteen minutes.

6

PUBLIC SPEAKING

We do a manageable number of nonpaid speaking engagements (panels, live interviews), which always lead to new clients. Keynote speaking involves a lot of time and preparation, so for that we require a fee.

7

PRODUCTS

2018 will be our year of launching multiple products. We are currently collaborating with Women in Travel (CIC) on a travel entrepreneurship e-course that will be sold through Udemy. We have been testing some photo-editing tools that we hope to launch in June. These two products have the potential to yield £4,000 [about $5,000] in a year. We're also in discussions on two books.

8

FREELANCE WRITING

We write for a variety of travel publications; however, we plan to do this less, so that we can put our time toward creating more products. Depending on the word count, we tend to earn anywhere from £150 to £350 [about $200 to $450] per article.

9

EVENTS

We currently collaborate with Melanin Travel to host Shades of Travel networking events targeted at ethnically diverse travel professionals. We hosted two events in 2017, and our most recent event sold out. We project earnings of £1,500 [about $1,950] this year.

10

AFFILIATE

We participate in a number of affiliate networks, including Amazon, Get Your Guide, Viator, Booking.com, and others. This is currently our lowest-yielding area only because of lack of development and focus. Over the next few months, we hope to earn a minimum of £300 [about $400] per month from our affiliations.

SEE THE
WORLD

FROM

TEACHER

TO

TRAVEL WRITER,
VLOGGER, TRAVEL
CHANNEL HOST

> *"If there was any time to do this pivot,
> it was now. It was a calculated gamble,
> but it was one that worked out for me."*

IT ALL STARTED WITH a college year abroad in France. Canadian-born Oneika Raymond loved the experience of living in Europe so much that she didn't want to go home. "I realized that I really loved to travel and it was something that I wanted to make a part of my life," says Oneika. "As soon as I got back to school in Canada, I was plotting for a way to go abroad again."

The ticket back to France was a job teaching English in a French high school after graduation. At the time, the requirements for teaching ESL abroad were a college degree and native fluency in English. Salaries range from $2,000 to $4,000 a month (sometimes tax free, depending on the country), so it was a perfect move for a new graduate.

After the year was up, Oneika decided to return to Canada to get her master's degree in teaching. With it, she knew, she could land a higher six-figure salary teaching English or French in British or American schools around the world.

Oneika spent the next ten years teaching in Mexico, Hong Kong, and London. During weekends and vacations she would explore different cities and countries. "I would simply look at places that were nearby and go to wherever was cheapest."

To chronicle her adventures for friends and family, Oneika started a blog in early 2005 called Oneika the Traveller. In the pre-Instagram era, the blog also allowed her to connect with other expats. When she realized that she had a following other than just her inner circle, she started writing advice for other people wanting to live, teach, or work abroad.

Six years later, while teaching in London, Oneika saw that she could leverage her large following to have brands sponsor her travel in return for exposure on her social media channels and site. Five years after that, she had to make a choice between maintaining her blog and teaching. "I moved to New York for my husband's job. I taught for ten years, and I was getting so many opportunities for travel. If there was any time to do this pivot, it was now. It was a calculated gamble, but it was one that worked out for me," says Oneika. "I make more money now. I'm a travel journalist, I still blog quite a bit. I get paid for my photography. I host for the Travel Channel with two series, *One Bag and You're Out* and *Big City, Little Budget*. I also work as a brand ambassador on campaigns and do on-air appearances."

Oneika's ease in front of the camera has been a boon to her career and a way to enhance her appeal to brands and TV. "I've always had a flair for the dramatic, and as a teenager I wanted to be a broadcast journalist," she reveals. As she goes into her second year as a freelancer, she only sees more opportunity. "I have been working toward this for a very long time. I love seeing new things every day. I love meeting people from all over the world. Now the world is my office."

4

GIVE
BACK

———

Pivot into Charity Work / *Raise Awareness* /
Run Toward Disaster /
Kick-Start a New Economy / *Make an Impact*

PURSUING A CAREER FOR THE SHEER JOY of it or the challenge or the perks will always fall short for you.

You need to feel that if you are going to work, there is a real purpose behind it. You want to see results that are life-changing, not measured simply by profits or sales or clicks or numbers. You want to see transformation in systems that aren't working. You want to create solutions. You want to enact lasting change.

This chapter spotlights people who came from vastly different backgrounds—human resources, commercial fishing, talent agencies, film, beauty, finance, and the NFL—but who all had that moment when they realized they wanted to fix, rescue, empower, heal, and impact lives. Their previous career just wasn't going to work anymore. They made sacrifices, sold their belongings, and said good-bye to hefty paychecks. They went back to school, found mentors, turned their lives over to God, learned how to heal, fight fires, save lives, and restore the oceans.

The world faces so many problems and so many chances to be a part of the solution.

Why not help out?

STEP IN
WHEN NO ONE ELSE DOES

SCOTT NEESON

FROM

—

PRESIDENT OF A MOVIE STUDIO

TO

CHILDREN'S CHARITY FOUNDER

SCOTT NEESON'S RISE FROM high school dropout to president of an international movie studio is compelling on its own. Then he walked away from his glamorous life and moved halfway around the world to live in a third-world country. Here's why.

Describe your life before you first visited Cambodia.

I didn't finish high school. By chance I got a job at a movie theater in Australia and worked my way up from there. I had what most people would consider the dream job as president of 20th Century Fox International. You fly first class, go to the Academy Awards, drive your

Porsche to the fanciest restaurants—it really is such a seductive lifestyle. For a boy from a working-class background, it was an absolute dream. People talk about how empty it must have been for me; it wasn't. When you're in it, you enjoy it.

What was the moment that changed everything for you?

I left 20th Century Fox for a job at Sony Pictures, and I had a five-week gap where I decided to travel through Southeast Asia. I spent a few days in Phnom Penh before going to Angkor Wat. I went to a local municipal landfill, and it was just unbelievable. The Steung Meanchey garbage dump is the size of about twenty football fields, incredibly hot, and the smell is unbearable. I saw about 1,500 children working there, gathering trash to sell in order to get enough money to eat. Some would burrow in pieces of plastic and sleep there at night.

How did you respond?

The reflexive response is to help. Without knowledge of the country or access to social resources, that meant stepping in to help a child who was walking past me. That single moment was the spark that started Cambodian Children's Fund. There was one girl I met, Srey Nich, she and her mother and sister were living on the garbage dump, and the sister was seriously ill with typhoid fever. I was in the corporate world, and what I could do really well was solve problems. Right then, I worked with her mother to get them a room to stay in, get Srey Nich into the public school, and get her sister to the hospital. I set up a system where I would send money to my local friend and he would give it to the mother each month to pay rent and buy food. It took about forty-five minutes and cost only $45 a month.

How did it evolve from helping Srey Nich to helping other children?

What stuck with me the most standing in the garbage dump was that no one else was helping at all. I went back to the hotel, and it kept on nagging at me that in one hour I had changed the course of this family's life. I didn't sleep that night. The next day I went back there with the same guy and found another four kids. I arranged for them to get to school and have a room to sleep in. This went on until I finally had to go back to Sony and start my job. By the time I left, I had committed to supporting eighteen children.

How did it feel to reenter your glamorous Hollywood life?

The experience in Cambodia had a really strong hold, and I did not want to go back to the Hollywood world. However, I was 45, and being in Los Angeles especially, you see some of the worst midlife crises, and I didn't want to become another one of those. I didn't want to throw away twenty-six years of work and six months later realize what a fool I had been. I made myself a promise not to do anything for twelve months. During those twelve months, I made eleven trips back to Cambodia. I made a lot of excuses to visit our Asian offices or travel with major actors going to Asia.

You were living a dual life, in a way. What made you choose one over the other?

I went from Tokyo to Phnom Penh after a premiere and went straight to the landfill. One of the grandmothers was in quite a fluster and took me to a more removed part of the dump. There was a small group of kids all in various stages of dying from typhoid fever. No one knew their background, and no one was going to take them to a hospital; they were just surviving themselves. The oldest was eight years old, and the youngest was three. They had been left by parents who no longer wanted them. And there it was. It was a really confronting moment.

At that very moment my cell phone rang, and it was my office in Los Angeles, which patched through an actor and his agent. They were very angry. They were leaving Tokyo, and our office had put a PlayStation on the G4, but our actor only had Xbox games with him, so he wouldn't get on the jet. He was carrying on about the fact that it was a long flight and "I specifically told everyone that I was an Xbox person." The actor made a comment like "My life wasn't meant to be this difficult." I calmed him down. I took care of it.

How did you respond?

When I hung up, all of my doubts and concerns, that sense of anxiety about wanting to move to Cambodia—they were gone. You want to have some sort of validation you're doing the right thing, and no one else is going to give it to you, but that moment was crystal clear. The life I was living appeared in the past, and standing on this garbage dump with dying children became my calling. No matter what your religion, there had to be some spiritual intervention. It took months to get out of my contract, for a number of reasons, but I did get out of it. I sold my house, sold a lot of my possessions, and I moved to Cambodia and started CCF to help children with education, family support, and community development. We are now working with over two thousand children.

What was the reaction of your friends and family when you said you were moving to Cambodia?

No one thought it was the right thing to do. No one really understood. The most common reaction was that I would be back in six months. My closest friends were cautioning me against it, saying, "Look at all you are leaving! You've got a beautiful girlfriend! You've got a car, a boat in the harbor! What are you doing?"

What were the biggest obstacles for you that first year in Cambodia?

I spent most days, seven days a week, on this horrendous garbage dump. I had asthma as a child, and my lungs weren't completely strong. Due to the burning toxins, I was often sick with bronchial infection. I got pneumonia once. But there was this dire anxiety to get these kids off this garbage dump. The ability to completely change the direction of a child's life was remarkable.

The first girl you met, Srey Nich, just graduated college with a degree in economics. What was that like for you?

I was almost in tears. It's not just about education. In Cambodia there is a real gender disparity. We can see how badly women are treated. There is a lack of any kind of dignity and understanding of what their rights are. We are really focused on having everyone, especially the boys, understand women's rights and emotional equality and that domestic violence is not okay. The twenty-six university graduates are not just well educated, but they have a real sense of giving back to society and combating poverty.

How would you describe your current life?

I was back in Los Angeles two months ago, I was sitting on the rooftop of a nice hotel, drinking a good Scotch and remembering, and realizing for the first time how much I had given up—having a good relationship or a relationship at all. Having a life where you aren't living amid abject poverty and acts of random violence, I miss that. But I feel so lucky to be where I am and to do what I do. The bigger question is about the overall life I've lived, and there is absolutely no way I regret that at all. I've made the greatest decision. I've lived a life that no one else has. I've found my dharma, I'm in my groove.

LISTEN, HEAL,
EMPOWER

TERRI COLE

FROM ▶ **TO**

TALENT AGENT PSYCHOTHERAPIST

WORKING WITH SUPERMODELS One of my early jobs was working at a commercial agency. I kept booking blond moms from Connecticut for detergent ads. It wasn't my thing. Then a talent agency hired me to work in its modeling division. It was a lot of negotiating contracts, thinking of everything that could happen and go wrong.

HELPING PEOPLE GET HEALTHY I stopped drinking when I was 21. So I had all these things happening in my life that made me know that there were more important things than a campaign for Pantene. What was I most lit up about? Getting someone into a drug treatment clinic, help-ing people with eating disorders, getting people help for depression. I referred dozens of models to therapy, trying to empower them. I was always trying to empower models, because it's such a horribly misogynistic business.

WANTING SOMETHING MORE MEANINGFUL I was dealing with divas like Naomi Campbell. That was the last deal that I did at the agency. I was like, *Okay, there has to be something better I could do with my life than making Naomi Campbell richer than she already is. This can't be my dharma. It can't be.*

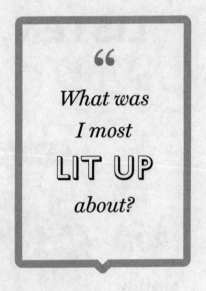

*What was
I most
LIT UP
about?*

GETTING A MASTER'S DEGREE I applied to NYU for my master's in clinical social work. I had gone to a bad undergraduate school to be a cheerleader. I did have good grades, though, and I knew I could get the school to understand the connection between what I was doing as a modeling agent and being a therapist. At the interview, I was able to tell stories of different interventions I had done and how I wanted to help women to have better lives. I think that's what got me in; I was super passionate about it.

BECOMING A THERAPIST My business was 90 percent actors, directors, sound people, lighting people, Broadway crew, and performers. I had the specialty of having been in entertainment, so I understood their lives. As a therapist, I could help them try to draw boundaries, teach them to speak authentically, teach them how to meditate.

REACHING MORE WOMEN Relatively early on, I also became a coach, because I just didn't fit into the therapy box. I work retainer-only now with a small group of clients, but I also run online courses. My work is all about female empowerment and really giving hope. One of my courses is Boundary Bootcamp, because this is such a huge issue, especially with women. I put out weekly videos and blogs. I do a lot of free stuff, really trying to reach people who can't afford to take my course. I want to reach as many women as I can.

THIS ISN'T A DRESS REHEARSAL I had a whole cancer experience in the middle of changing my career from agent to therapist. It had a lot to do with me just waking up and realizing that living on caffeine, smoking cigarettes, and traveling all the time wasn't my best life. Having a cancer diagnosis—and I went through it twice and had two surgeries—it really did shift the risks I was willing to take. It really woke me up to wanting to add value, to know time is of the essence. What if you lived like you were dying? What different choices would you make? What stuff would you not complain about? What pettiness would you perhaps let go of if you really remembered that all of this is a gift? Every experience, all of the lessons, all of the joy and the sorrows, all of it is a gift.

PIVOT INTO
CHARITY
WORK

Adam Braun left Wall Street to start two educational ventures designed to help people transform their lives: Pencils of Promise, an organization that builds schools and educational programs around the world, and MissionU, a one-year program that reimagines college. If you want to focus your career on giving back, here are his top five pieces of advice.

1

BRANCH OUT

True self-discovery begins where your comfort zone ends. That might mean traveling, changing your circle of relationships, or changing your hobbies and interests. Exposing yourself to something that you might have never thought you were interested in is the fastest way to discover who you are.

2

UNDERSTAND HOW CHARITIES AND BUSINESSES WORK BEFORE STARTING YOUR OWN

Not everyone has to be a founder; if anything, you deal with a lot of administrative minutiae that is not as glamorous as people think. Find an organization that you deeply believe in, and try to find a way to work with them. At the very least you will learn from the experience, and that will help make you more confident when you go to start your own thing.

IGNORE THE NAYSAYERS (THERE WILL BE MANY)

In the early days it is about having the fortitude to keep working on something that most people will tell you is not going to work. Most people said it was going to be impossible in 2008 to raise money to build schools in rural parts of the developing world when the economy was imploding. I was 24, turning 25, with very little money myself and my friends all losing their jobs, but I did it.

SET REALISTIC FINANCIAL GOALS

With any new venture there are challenges in making sure you can continue to fund-raise in a successful way every year. There is pressure to outdo yourself, to raise more capital than the previous year, and that can oftentimes be challenging, especially as the economy can ebb and flow.

HIRE PEOPLE WHO HAVE THE SAME MISSION YOU DO

Early on, you have to be very deliberate and intentional about the culture that you create within your company and organization. You have to put that culture front and center in a myriad of ways and try to find people who can augment and accelerate it through their own unique contributions. In our interview process I am very up front about that culture, and I ask, "What are the three values that you would personally want to bring to our culture that you care most about?" The candidate's answers are just as important as what is on his or her résumé.

RAISE
AWARENESS

FROM
—
NFL FOOTBALL
PLAYER

TO
—
ARTIST, AUTHOR,
TEACHER,
COMMUNITY
ACTIVIST

BEING AN ARTIST AND AN ATHLETE Art has always been a big part of who I am. I won an art competition and did my first commissioned mural for the state of Maryland when I was 11 years old. When I was 13, I took college-level art courses on scholarship. I double majored in integrative arts and broadcast journalism at Penn State. With football, I started at 5 and went on to play in the NFL. I was drafted a year early to the Buffalo Bills.

DISTINGUISHING REALITY FROM DREAMS Ever since I was a kid, I said, "I am going to play in the NFL, and I'm going to be a famous artist." I always had that plan. I saw myself experiencing certain milestones in the NFL, but then you actually make it there and realize that it isn't what you thought it was going to be. When we're younger, we think of only the money, the fame, the opportunity that millions of people would love to have, but what you don't think about is the microscope you live under. You don't think about how everything you say is judged, the mental toll it takes on you, that you don't get a chance to participate in the lives of your family and the people in your community in the way you would like to.

GIVING BACK When I was growing up, all the athletes I idolized were guys who were iconic because of who they were outside of the athletic arena. Guys like Muhammad Ali, Jack Johnson, Tommie Smith, John Carlos, Kareem Abdul-Jabbar, people who used their platform and their talents to uplift and build their communities.

LEAVING THE NFL I played in the NFL for five years. Ultimately I just got to the point where I could no longer justify, aside from being paid, why I was still playing. I was released by the Cincinnati Bengals before the start of what was supposed to be my last year under that contract. My agent was lining up six or seven different visits to other teams. The morning I was supposed to fly out, I was overwhelmed with emotion and I couldn't bring myself to get on the plane. I was like, *Nothing in you wants to do this.* When your heart isn't in it, people can tell. I asked myself, *What is going to bring me that happiness?* The answer was both my artwork and the work I was doing in my community.

PAINTING AND WRITING I took three months where I did nothing but lock myself in the studio. I painted. I wrote. I did my photography. My book, *Art Activism*, started to come together even though I didn't know what I was writing at the time.

BREAKING INTO THE ART WORLD I did a lot of hard work and due diligence, trying to break into the professional art world as a former athlete. I understood that even though I had been an artist my whole life, none of that was going to matter to people who were meeting me for the first time. They were going to say, "Oh, this is an athlete who just decided he wants to be an artist." I put in that work of really mastering my craft, finding my voice, and figuring out how to build my brand to the point where I could sustain myself off of my art and other entrepreneurial businesses. It took me a few years to find that balance. Last year all of it started coming together.

GIVING BACK THROUGH TEACHING I've been teaching arts and literacy three days a week for the past year in the public school system. I teach every student in a West Baltimore elementary school on a rotating schedule. The other two days I work on my art, travel, and do speaking engagements.

CREATING AWARENESS Before I put a video on social media showing my students trying to learn in a classroom without heat, I was tweeting about the fact that our students had no heat. When I was tweeting, people were blaming Republicans, Democrats, Trump, the mayor, saying, "You should be mad at this person or this person." My response was basically "To hell with that. I'm furious with everyone. Everyone connected with this system could find it in themselves to say, 'What can we do to fix it?'" I put those videos out because I thought no human being with a soul could see what my kids are dealing with, the environment they are expected to learn in, and not in some way feel some empathy or responsibility to do something.

EFFECTING CHANGE I was able to connect with Samierra Jones and Valerie Arum and start the Operation Heat campaign. We raised more than $85,000 in a three-week period. With that money we were able to purchase space heaters, hats, coats, and gloves for more than fifty schools in the Baltimore area. We partnered with Amazon to provide every single kid at my school with a new coat. Two contracted companies reached out to donate new heating systems to my school. God willing, we will have it installed by the end of the school year. I'm not going to lie and act like we fixed the problem. Things are just as bad as they were in most of these schools, but we've been able to get much-needed resources into the hands of the kids and teachers. We've been able to raise a national dialogue.

DOING THE GREATEST GOOD Everything I've wanted to do with my life, I've done. I still have a lot of goals. I'm trying to do the greatest good that I can do. I have a responsibility to speak up on issues that are marginalized and forgotten. I have a following of people who don't see themselves represented in media or the art scene or in venues they were always told were not for them. I happen to be somebody who is invited to those tables and asked to be at those meetings. I have a responsibility to use that platform to benefit my community. I try to be an example through my life of how one can use their talents, skills, and whatever platform they have to create a better world rather than just complain. We can critique culture and society, but there is also the responsibility of being part of the change.

RUN TOWARD
DISASTER

NICOLE LATERRA

DAY JOB

HAIRDRESSER,
SALON OWNER

SIDE GIG

VOLUNTEER EMT
AND FIREFIGHTER

BORN TO DO HAIR My mother was always a hairdresser, so growing up I was always around it. I knew I had a God-given talent to do it. I knew it would be great for my kids to be able to bring them to work and make my own hours. It just fell into place. I never explored any other options.

SPREADING SUNSHINE I love what I do: making people happy and beautiful and making them feel good about themselves. That was the main reason I got into owning my salon, to make people smile.

FEELING A NEED TO HELP I have been in many situations where people got hurt around me—a diabetic emergency or someone breaking their arm. Other people would get scared, look on, or run away, and I would find myself running to help. I had this need to fix the situation and make them feel better. I wanted to help even though I didn't know how, which is why I went into the volunteer field to become an emergency medical technician.

GOING BACK TO SCHOOL I took an eight-month course to become certified as an EMT because I thought that would have the most impact on my local community. I looked for classes that would fit my schedule around running my business and being a mom.

GOING INTO THE FIRE In Cromwell, Connecticut, we are a combination fire and EMS department, which means we have both career personnel and volunteer personnel working in the same department. I started as an EMT and worked my way up to lieutenant, but I wanted to do more. I knew I could do more. Being on scene at a fire and realizing *I could do that, too! I could run into a burning building and help somebody and put the fire out and do it just as well as the guys.*

TRAINING TO BECOME A FIREFIGHTER I have four kids, and at the time that I did firefighter training, my twins were four months old. I don't really know how I did that! I think I just knew it was something I had to do. I went to school for six months, again on nights and weekends. I made myself do it. I am so glad I did.

TAKING ON A DANGEROUS JOB It was a little nerve-racking, and I was scared at first. But once you go into school, you know how to control the situation and make it better; I was like, *I can do this*. The more training I had and the more I was around my fire department family—I just excelled.

BEING A FEMALE FIREFIGHTER In my department, there are only three female firefighters out of one hundred. I think there are a lot of stereotypes that women can't do the same job, but not so much in my department. The men on my team know that I can do the job and do it correctly. I have their back in any situation, and they have mine.

KEEPING BOTH GIGS If I'd found firefighting first, I might have done only that, but I have two really great careers and I don't want to give up one because they balance each other out. The department actually pays us per incident, so it is a little extra income, which helps, too.

SHOWING MY KIDS THAT THEY CAN DO ANYTHING I love being able to show my kids that if they put their mind to it, they can do whatever they want to. It also means a lot to be able to do this job as a woman and to show my kids and other women that they can do this job. Being able to help someone on the worst day of their life is what makes me want to do this.

HELP PEOPLE

"Most people don't realize that 70 percent of firefighters in the US are volunteers," says Kimberly Quiros, director of communications for the National Volunteer Fire Council. Whether you want to save lives or help out behind the scenes, here are three ways to get started.

CONNECT WITH YOUR LOCAL FIRE STATION

"With increasing call volumes and services, departments need more people to step up to serve their community in this extraordinary and rewarding way," Quiros says. To see what volunteer opportunities are available, check out the National Volunteer Fire Council's website, https://www.nvfc.org/.

HELP OUT IN OTHER WAYS

There are plenty of additional opportunities to help out. Fire departments need fire prevention educators, administrators, and fund-raisers—all of whom are essential to keeping the operation running smoothly.

BECOME AN EMT

EMTs are often the first responders in medical emergencies. Basic training takes anywhere from five months to two years, plus a background check and certification exam. You are required to be recertified every two years.

KICK-START A
NEW ECONOMY
AND RESTORE THE
OCEANS

BREN SMITH

FROM — COMMERCIAL FISHERMAN ▸ **TO** — RESTORATIVE OCEAN FARMER

RAISED FISHING I grew up in Newfoundland in a tiny fishing village. It was what we think of the great side of fishing, the romance of it, people cooking squid on the beach and out jigging for cod in small boats. It was very community based, kids selling cod door-to-door for a penny.

FOLLOWING THE FISH You chase the jobs, and for me they were in Gloucester and Lynn, Massachusetts, with lobster and tuna. Later, I went where every young fisherman dreams to go, which is the Bering

Sea for cod and crab. The cod was going to McDonald's for their fish sandwich. It was the height of industrial food production and harvesting of the most unsustainable and unhealthy food on the planet.

DEALING WITH THE DEPLETED OCEANS In 1994, the cod stocks crashed, and that was a huge wake-up call. The hyperlocal, sustainable form of fishery was decimated. Thousands of people thrown out of work, canneries completely empty, a culture hollowed out really quickly because of ecological devastation. It was clear that what we are doing in terms of food production is not the right path—not just environmentally but for jobs. What it didn't answer was, what should we be doing to be sustainable? To completely revamp the food system in a serious way, what are the solutions?

DISCOVERING THE PROMISE (AND LIE) OF FARMED SALMON I headed back to Newfoundland to do salmon agriculture. I was told that that was the answer to help feed the planet, create jobs, and help reduce the pressure on fish stocks. That was a false bill of goods. It was pesticides, antibiotics, and pollution. We were growing neither fish nor food. In 1995, I left there, disillusioned.

DEVELOPING A SUSTAINABLE FOOD MODEL I read an article in the paper that New Haven was opening up shellfishing grounds for the first time in hundreds of years to attract young fishermen like me. It was really the oysters that shifted my whole identity from hunter to farmer. What the oysters taught me is that we can have a restorative economy and food system. Oysters, shellfish, and seaweed use no fresh water, no fish feed, no fertilizers, no land, while restoring our ecosystem. Filtering out nitrogen and carbon, building reefs, providing storm surge protection—oysters are agents of restoration.

ADAPTING TO CLIMATE CHANGE After seven years of oyster farming, I got hit by Hurricane Irene, then Hurricane Sandy. That was when I had to take the lessons learned from oysters and try to apply them and reimagine farms in the era of climate change. That was when I moved the farm off the bottom of the seafloor. Now I use hurricane-proof anchors and a rope scaffolding system in the ocean.

FARMING THE OCEAN I wrap kelp weed that I grow in my hatchery around those lines, and it grows vertically downward. I grow mussels below on a second horizontal line. Once I harvest the kelp and the mussels, I put scallops in, so I can have a rotational crop. The clams I put down in the mud with oysters in cages on the seafloor. I also grow a form of red seaweed called Gracilaria, and we harvest sea salt off our ground. Thimble Island Ocean Farm attracts over 150 species of marine life.

MITIGATING RISK Growing multiple species spreads the risk; if one crop fails, I add another. It creates a year-round farm. The trouble for land-based farmers is that affording land requires incredible capital costs. That is why 91 percent of farmers in 2012 in the United States lost money.

LEASING OCEAN RIGHTS We lease the farm from the town or state. It's $25 to $50 an acre per year. We don't own the water rights; the ocean is common, and we want to keep it that way. What we do own is the right to grow shellfish and seaweed. We own a process right but not a property right.

DEVELOPING A BETTER ECONOMIC MODEL There are minimal capital requirements, which allows for really fast replication of the farms. At Greenwave we have ten farms starting up this year; we will have twenty-five by next year. The economics of this are game-changing.

You need $10,000 for the setup costs. Then it's two to three full-time jobs, five to seven seasonal jobs, and the profit for the farmer is between $100,000 and $150,000.

LOVING KELP Kelp is one of the fastest-growing plants on Earth. It can be used for so many things: food, fertilizer, animal feed, pharmaceuticals, cosmetics, and biofuel. There are over 250 types. It's not just kelp, though; there are 10,000 edible plants in the ocean. Kelp is just the gateway drug to a whole new way of eating. All of the nutritional benefits we need are available in the ocean in sea greens and bivalves. We are really at a peak of culinary enlightenment in the United States, we have all these creative chefs who are experimenting to make them delicious.

DEVELOPING A NEW WAY TO FARM, A NEW WAY TO EAT The exciting thing is that we are starting from scratch. This is our chance to do agriculture right, to make sure that our seas aren't privatized, to make sure low-income people can afford leases, to make sure we lift up entire communities and create new professions. If you want to lift up the middle class, this is how to do it.

INNOVATING The world is a pretty depressing and discouraging place, so I want to be part of the folks coming up with the solutions. The interesting thing about climate change is that it's forcing innovation. Our backs are against the wall, and we have to reformat pretty much everything we do as an economy and a society. That's what is really exciting, being part of the solution-based economy.

LET GOD BE YOUR BOSS

CARLYE HUGHES

FROM

REGIONAL DIRECTOR OF TRAINING AND DEVELOPMENT FOR A HOTEL BRAND

TO

BISHOP OF THE EPISCOPAL CHURCH

> *"Part of what I do is help people discover how God is calling them."*

CARLYE HUGHES WASN'T LOOKING for a new job. She had a successful career working in human resources, specializing in hotel employee training and development, but one question from someone at her church in New York City changed her life's trajectory: "Have you ever thought about ordained ministry?" She hadn't, but something about the idea made her reflect on it, made her imagine an entirely different life for herself. "I just had a sense it was something I needed to spend some time thinking about," Carlye says. "Some people may say that is the Holy Spirit. It just resonated."

Carlye spent a year reflecting on the concept of life in the ministry before she went further with it. "I had to do some thinking, some praying, reading, and just kind of letting myself get used to the idea." The path to ministry in the Episcopal Church is a long one. On average, the ordination process takes almost two years. There are months of discussions within your parish and months at the diocesan level. "Then you wait to hear from your bishop, who decides whether they feel you have a call to ordained ministry," explains Carlye. That is all before three years of seminary school.

During the time before she would know if she was chosen, Carlye learned to release her worry. "You have absolutely no control, so that is where you learn what you're made of. Are you going to worry your way all the way through it? Are you going to sit and say, 'I'm in this with God?'" At one point, she talked to a friend who was a Pentecostal preacher who had some wise insights. "She said, 'Honey, I wouldn't worry about that at all. If it is something you are supposed to do, God is going to drive a big bus up to your door and say, "Will you get on the priest bus?"' I always had that image that either the priest bus was going to pick me up or it was going to keep driving."

After Carlye was chosen, she left her life in New York behind to go to seminary in Virginia. She had financial aid, and her sponsoring congregation took up a collection to lower the cost of her education. After seminary, she went to a parish in Peekskill, New York, for five years before becoming rector at Trinity Episcopal Church in Fort Worth, Texas, and in May 2018 she was elected bishop of the Diocese of Newark, the first woman and first African American to be elected to that post.

Carlye loves the wide reach of her job, from managing the direction of the church to supporting parishioners. "I like being the person who helps people figure out the direction the church is going in, kind of uncovering the vision together. I am very much a collaborator. I don't really set a vision and tell people 'This is true north.' We discover together which direction is true north. Part of what I do is help people discover how God is calling them to be a part of that vision."

> "
> *I had to do some thinking, some praying, reading . . .*

MAKE AN
IMPACT

FROM ▶

TEACHER

TO ▶

**VENTURE
PHILANTHROPIST**

> *"I believe that those who are closest to the
> problem are closest to the solution."*

I**T WAS THE EXPERIENCE** of teaching high school English in a struggling West Philadelphia public school that made Aaron Walker realize that good teaching alone wasn't enough to create real change for students. The school lacked a library and basic resources. The largest high school class was ninth grade, the smallest was twelfth. He saw how issues outside of school such as poverty, hunger, and violence created roadblocks for students. "When I step back and look at it, the responsibility put on teachers to overcome all these other systemic things going on in our society, it just felt unsustainable. How does a teacher reach a kid when he cannot think because he hasn't eaten?" he asks. "It propelled me to figure out where I could make the biggest social change."

Aaron enrolled in law school, believing that becoming a civil rights lawyer would be the way to create change. But the reality of student loans led him to take a job as a corporate lawyer. "In law school there is this direct path to working for a law firm. They make it so easy for you, and you're in so much debt that you have to have a really strong emotional fortitude to say, 'I am not going to follow the herd,'" he explains. The move to corporate law was lucrative, and in less than two years, he paid off 90 percent of his debt. "That gave me the freedom to do the things I wanted to do."

> *We are a **strong beginning** for these entrepreneurs, who often have additional hurdles because of their race, gender, or background.*

Aaron then refocused his quest to help students and took a job as portfolio director at the Fund for Public Schools, the venture philanthropy arm of the New York City Department of Education under Mayor Michael Bloomberg. It was an opportunity to learn about entrepreneurship, fund-raising, and how to find new ways to impact education. However, Aaron noticed a flaw in the system. "I was particularly appalled and somewhat disappointed that a lot of the new ideas for communities of color were not led by people of color. It suggested that folks of color were only the problem, not the

solution," he says. "I believe that those who are closest to the problem are closest to the solution. We have a set of experiences that I think puts us closer to solving these issues. I decided I wanted to try to do something about it. That was the impetus for starting Camelback."

The company Aaron founded is Camelback Ventures, a hybrid of venture capital and what Aaron calls venture philanthropy, focused on helping underrepresented entrepreneurs launch social impact start-ups primarily around education. A previous start-up idea failed after Aaron spent too much time working on a proposal for investors, so this time he didn't wait for permission or funding, he just got started.

Aaron connected with new entrepreneurs who needed mentors. He worked with them for four months, helping them turn their ideas into real businesses. He then used the success stories to land investors. "I wasn't putting a concept paper in front of potential investors. Instead, I talked about the work I did with entrepreneurs in our pilot year. I was able to say, 'Look what we did, see the progress that we

made, imagine the progress we could make with even more funding.'"
It worked, and Aaron raised over a million dollars.

Institutions such as AT&T, the Walton Family Foundation, and the Bill & Melinda Gates Foundation are investors in Camelback. In turn, each year Camelback invests $40,000 into each venture of a dozen entrepreneurs, providing support with three things Aaron believes are essential: coaching, capital, and connections. "The idea is that we are a strong beginning for these entrepreneurs, who often have additional hurdles because of their race, gender, or background. We put them on a path to be investment-ready for the fund-raising that will happen beyond us."

So far, Camelback has helped more than thirty fellows launch their education initiatives. Of the Camelback fellows, 90 percent are people of color, and over half are women. One success story is former Camelback fellow Jonathan Johnson, who just launched Rooted School in New Orleans to prepare high school graduates for tech jobs. "It is incredible to see ninth graders doing 3-D modeling and earning a certification that would make them eligible for jobs that pay $50,000 a year," says Aaron.

Aaron's background as a teacher gives him insight into many of the education initiatives he backs and also helps in his role as mentor. "I am still a teacher at heart. I get the most thrill out of seeing others succeed, to see what our fellows have done in the early years is exciting," he says. "These last four years have proven to me what I always knew—that genius is equally distributed but access is not."

"

HAVING A CANCER DIAGNOSIS—
AND I WENT THROUGH IT TWICE
AND HAD TWO SURGERIES—IT
REALLY DID SHIFT THE RISKS I WAS
WILLING TO TAKE. IT REALLY WOKE
ME UP TO WANTING TO ADD VALUE,
TO KNOW TIME IS OF THE ESSENCE.
WHAT IF YOU LIVED LIKE YOU WERE
DYING? WHAT DIFFERENT CHOICES
WOULD YOU MAKE? WHAT STUFF
WOULD YOU NOT COMPLAIN ABOUT?
WHAT PETTINESS WOULD YOU
PERHAPS LET GO OF IF YOU REALLY
REMEMBERED THAT ALL OF THIS
IS A GIFT? EVERY EXPERIENCE,
ALL OF THE LESSONS, ALL OF THE
JOY AND THE SORROWS, ALL OF IT
IS A GIFT.

TERRI COLE

"Listen, Heal, Empower," page 137

5

FOLLOW
YOUR
BLISS

*Open a Bookstore / Relive Your Youth /
Get Paid to Talk Sports / Work with Your Hands /
Leave Your Job, Then Go Back*

AS CAREER ADVICE, the idea of following your passion is somewhat misguided. For starters, it implies that we all have only one thing that we are interested in or one thing that we're good at. That the right career is sort of like a soul mate. That you will succeed only when you pair up with the career you were "meant" to be pursuing.

For most people, careers and hobbies or passions don't really line up that way. What you are interested in one decade or one year might change drastically the next. You also might love something, but pursuing it might not be the best job for you.

The majority of people in this chapter are doing what they love, for sure, but they didn't necessarily know what that was from the start. What became their career wasn't necessarily their sole passion, just one aspect of their lives.

The career leapers featured here found their new careers from wanting to see an idea become reality, trying to contribute to their community, or tapping into what lit them up as a teenager. Their new career may not last forever, it may not be the only thing that does that, but the impetus led them down an exciting new path.

Where will yours lead?

OPEN A
BOOKSTORE

NOËLLE SANTOS

FROM ▸

HUMAN
RESOURCES
PAYROLL
ADMINISTRATOR

TO

BOOKSTORE
OWNER

WANT TO OPEN A BOOKSTORE? Here's how Noëlle Santos did it.

STEP 1: FIND A CAUSE WORTH FIGHTING FOR It all started because I was pissed off that there was only one bookstore in the Bronx. It was a Barnes & Noble located all the way in the northeast Bronx, and you couldn't even get there by public transportation. I love reading, so I wanted to bring a second bookstore to the borough, something that was more accessible, that reflected the community and provided opportunities.

STEP 2: COME UP WITH A GAME PLAN, THEN REDO IT I had a good job in human resources, and I have a master's degree in business/HR. I never imagined myself as a bookseller. I thought the bookstore could be a side hustle. I would get a store manager. I would continue to work in HR, maybe take a little leave, be an absentee owner, get somebody who was more bookish. Then I grew up! I realized that's not how any of this works. It became clear that if this bookstore was going to happen, I had to do it.

STEP 3: NETWORK I signed up for a Paz & Associates retreat in Florida called Owning a Bookstore. It was a weeklong course where you learn what it takes, what you need to do, and if bookstore ownership is something that complements your skill set. There I heard about a contest called the New York StartUP! Business Plan Competition from one of my classmates.

STEP 4: GET SOME MENTORS I ended up coming in second place in the competition. I beat out 358 other entries for tech companies, start-ups, inventions, and all types of businesses. They gave me resources, workshops, and an adviser to help me learn to write a business plan. I had an advantage because my bachelor's degree is in accounting so I know all about numbers and budgets. One of my insecurities was *Am I bookish enough for this?* But all the booksellers I met told me they wish they'd had the business background first and then they could have learned the rest later. That made me feel a little braver.

STEP 5: UP YOUR GAME In 2016, the property owners didn't renew the lease for Barnes & Noble. It closed, leaving the Bronx—home to 1.5 million people—with no bookstore. I knew I had to make my bookstore happen.

STEP 6: CREATE BUZZ Before I asked for a dollar on crowdfunding, I was building my personal brand on social media. I was associated with books and starting intellectual conversations online. I blogged about every trial and tribulation. Everybody was emotionally invested in my journey and this dream. You need to be storytelling and doing it well in advance.

STEP 7: STAND OUT FROM THE CROWD The title of my crowdfunding campaign was "Let's Bring a Goddamn Bookstore to the Bronx!" I was unorthodox in my messaging. I went in with the intention of *I don't have a lot of time, I need to go viral.* Instead of talking, I did my pitch in a rap. I broke all the rules. I got all these emails from professional fund-raisers saying "You've made a big mistake! Do your fund-raising in December, when people are giving." But I know my community has income during income tax season. So I went with it.

STEP 8: RAISE MONEY Originally my plan was to raise $40,000, but a friend said, "If you set your goal at $40K, then you're only going to put in $40K worth of work. Set it at $100,000 and I know you will do it." I decided on $70,000, and then a couple of seconds before I set it up, I changed it to $100,000. I hit Send, and I was like, *Oh, my God, what did I just do?* The campaign raised over $160,000.

STEP 9: ENVISION WHAT YOU WANT TO CREATE I have been complaining my whole life that there is nothing to do in the Bronx. We take our dollars outside of the borough. We get a little education and get out of the hood. I wanted to build something here and inspire others to build businesses that are for us and by us. It is really hard to give opportunities to local people in a corporate structure; you have all these levels of chain to go through.

STEP 10: ADD A TWIST The Lit Bar is a combination of bookstore and wine bar, a gathering space for book lovers. The whole hybrid model is popping up a lot more, business owners are getting more savvy, booksellers are getting smarter. Where independent booksellers win is by becoming community spaces. I can't think of a better way to bond in communities than to have a glass of wine and talk about literature.

STEP 11: SIGN A LEASE My neighborhood is gentrifying, so finding a space was the hardest part. The neighborhood was recently rezoned from industrial use to mixed use, so a lot of the places I found needed a ton of work. Then the nice spaces were charging an exorbitant amount of money, waiting for affluent tenants. Before I raised the money, property owners didn't want to talk to me—I am a woman, I am black, I am Latina, I am from the South Bronx trying to open a bookstore in 2017—I had every stigma against me. The people who did talk to me were condescending: "You're never going to raise this money." But when that crowdfunding campaign popped and it went crazy in the media, I had property owners lining up. Then I had some options!

The very first broker I reached out to reached back out to me. He said, "I never forgot about you. There is a brand-new building that is right for you." He told me the owners were already familiar with my story and they wanted a bookstore and they wanted me to do it. I met with them and gave them a presentation. The next day they gave me a draft of the lease. I had been so depressed trying to find a space, it took so long. Then it all turned around. I've got 1,600 square feet with 600 feet of basement space. I quit my job in HR. I'm all in. I'm ready.

HOW I GOT HERE

Noëlle Santos's path to bookstore owner

SUMMER CAMP COUNSELOR

JUNIOR HIGH SCHOOL DANCE TEACHER

MOVIE THEATER CASHIER

CAR DEALERSHIP FILING CLERK

BANK TELLER

ADMINISTRATIVE ASSISTANT

OFFICE MANAGER

SEX TOY COMPANY OWNER

PAYROLL AND HR ADMINISTRATOR

FISCAL DIRECTOR

HR AND PAYROLL MANAGER AND DIRECTOR

BOOKSTORE/ WINE BAR OWNER, LITERARY ACTIVIST, SPEAKER, AND CONTRIBUTOR TO *PUBLISHERS WEEKLY*

ENVISION YOUR
FUTURE
(ALONG WITH EVERYONE ELSE'S)

ANGIE BANICKI

FROM › PUBLICIST

TO ‹ TAROT CARD READER

> *"It wasn't like reading tarot was something I always wanted to do. It really just happened."*

ANGIE BANICKI WAS NEVER a believer in psychics or tarot cards. She didn't even read her horoscope. When her former boss would dish to colleagues on his yearly psychic session, she would leave to grab a coffee. She just wasn't interested.

Angie was an entertainment publicist in Hollywood connecting celebrities with brands and events. Her life was an endless loop of going to brand meetings, mixing it up with stars, partying, and traveling. After a decade, however, she became disillusioned with the surface nature of her job. With her thirtieth birthday looming, she decided to quit. "I tend to always do things drastically. I had to shut it down and reset," she says. "A lot of publicists can get bitter. I didn't like the person I was becoming."

Angie wanted something less exhausting, less superficial, more meaningful. She just couldn't figure out what that was and planned to freelance consult for brands she had previously worked with to buy some time to figure it out. Her break was short-lived. "I got sucked right back into PR," she says. "I think I wasn't really ready to give up my identity. I just convinced myself it was different because I was doing it on my own."

Soon after, however, her life began to veer in a surprising new direction. It all started with a deck of Prada tarot cards a friend gave Angie as a gag birthday gift. On a whim, she took the cards to parties to "read" friends. She wasn't expecting anything to be accurate. Then her predictions started coming true. "I would say off the cuff, 'Oh, you just lost your job, but you have two job offers.' And someone would be shocked and say, 'How did you know that?' Or they would call me later and say, 'Angie, it turned out exactly as you said!'"

Despite her accuracy, Angie chalked it up to coincidence. "I had trouble believing it, because I didn't believe in tarot cards before," she says. "It wasn't like reading tarot was something I always wanted to do. It really just happened."

The tarot cards seemed to tap into something cosmic. Angie started having dreams and premonitions. She correctly predicted a complication with a friend's birth, including that the baby would be fine after ten days. In another dream, she saw that her brother would have two accidents on a trip to India.

Word got out, and Angie's phone began ringing. She did quick readings for friends and then for friends of friends. When someone suggested she charge for the readings, she was hesitant. "When you love something so much, it feels weird to ask someone to give you money."

Angie quickly noticed a massive disparity between how she felt when she did her PR work and how she felt when she did a reading. "I would feel elated that I just helped someone make a decision or know that everything would be okay. My intentions are always to help someone. It just made me care less and less about the PR work."

> "
> *It was such a transition of* I AM HAPPIER NOW. I DON'T NEED ALL THE THINGS I THOUGHT I DID.

Although making the switch sounded great in theory, when she did make the move, the financial reality was problematic. Her PR clients had been paying her $10,000 a month, and her tarot clients paid only $200 a session. To make it work, she moved into a smaller place, stopped buying new clothes and going out to eat, and lived off of her savings until she could increase her income. "What's interesting is, I didn't miss spending any of that money. It was such a transition of *I am happier now. I don't need all the things I thought I did.*"

Despite her marketing background, Angie wasn't confident announcing to the world that she was going to be a professional tarot card reader. "Every job I've ever had, I was always so excited to send out that email about what I was doing next, but this was the first time

I didn't do that. My experience was PR and marketing, but I couldn't PR and market myself," she says. Angie was afraid what other people's perception of her new career would be, especially by her old crowd, who couldn't understand why she would leave a financially lucrative and glamorous career. "A few people from my past were like, 'What did she do?'"

Angie noticed a subtle pulling back of friendships, invites not arriving, and people she thought were close avoiding her. "I realized I had a lot of superficial friendships. It was a wake-up call," she explains. "I think this translates into any career change, but previously I had a certain power. It felt like once I stepped away from all that, I could see what was real." Her close friends stuck by her, championing her new career and spreading the word.

It turned out that Angie didn't need to do a big marketing push to be successful. She built her brand on word of mouth and, after three years, began making her former PR salary. She currently charges $400 per reading. She also reads at the same type of brand events she used to put together, counting *W* magazine and Dior as clients. Angie likes reading for partygoers much more than when she had to work at those parties as a PR rep. "I love being able to help people. The joy I feel after time with someone is unlike anything I felt working with big brands. It is so rewarding."

RELIVE YOUR YOUTH

MARJORIE GUBELMANN

FROM

CANDLE
COMPANY OWNER

TO

DJ

IWAS HAVING SUNDAY LUNCH in my apartment with one of my very good friends, Mickey Boardman, the editorial director of *Paper* magazine. We were talking about all of these young girl DJs in the world and this is how the conversation went:

ME: I was actually a DJ in college in the eighties.
MICKEY: You were not!
ME: Yes, I was! My DJ name was Mad Marj.
MICKEY: You are going to DJ my birthday party.
ME: Are you kidding me? I haven't done this in twenty years! I was in a basement talking to myself into a microphone with records. I have no idea what I'm doing. It was such a long time ago.

MICKEY: No one knows what they are doing! I'll have a man there to help you. Just wear a fancy dress. Just show up!

ME: I'll do it for fifteen minutes.

I was 42 and a single mom with a candle company. That was the official start of my career as a DJ.

Mickey's party was at a downtown hotel with a few hundred people. My fifteen minutes turned into three hours. I had the time of my life. It is so cliché, but I felt it! It was like, *I love this!* I felt like I was a teenager again. I loved how it made me feel. I loved how I made people feel by playing music that made them dance. You feed off of that energy.

The next day people were calling me for jobs, which was fantastic because I needed them. I had gone through a not pleasant divorce that had cleaned me out considerably financially. The jobs I needed came, but something in my head said, *Don't do it yet. You need to go to school. You can't be a fraud.* I didn't want to be that person who didn't know what they were doing. I've never been a very proactive student, I always looked for shortcuts, I was never prepared, but now I wanted to go back to school.

I called a friend of mine in the music business and said, "Do not laugh and don't ask me any questions, but I need to go to DJ school." He told me there was only one place to go, Scratch DJ Academy in the East Village, which was cofounded by Run-DMC's Jam Master Jay.

I called and enrolled. I told one friend only. I figured if it didn't work out, no one would know. I thought for sure it was a phase. Everybody in my class was 19. I could have been their parent! I think musically they were like, 'Oh, God, there she goes!'" I was playing Madonna, and they were playing house music. I knew that there would be no one who fit the box of me in the class, but I liked that. In the end, we were all there for the same thing.

I went to school for a good six months. Becoming a DJ is way harder than it looks. Even six years later, I go for lessons when there is new software that I need to learn. There are a lot of technical parts to being a DJ. Today your music is in a computer, which is your library. You have two turntables, but there is no music on the records, but it is how you blend your songs, how you start a song and how you end a song. When I did it in the eighties, there were actually records with songs on them on the turntables, so it took a long time for me to figure out.

My career took off from word of mouth with people saying "Can you believe that Marjorie is a DJ?" I think the swing from the perception that I was this uptown lady and now I am in the DJ booth, the whole juxtaposition, no one could believe it. Word got out, and it trickled down. I have some amazing friends who are my biggest promoters, which has been really helpful. I have been around New York and the social scene for a long time, and you can't discount that it has helped.

I think in my thirties I would have been too insecure, but at 42, I was at an age where I didn't care what people thought. You have to be at that junction in your life to do these big changes. And you know what? Everyone is psyched for me. My son is the most proud. He loves that I am a DJ.

I work for a lot of fashion, beauty, and jewelry companies such as Dolce & Gabbana, Estée Lauder, Kiehl's, Tory Burch. I do a lot of corporate events. I am a freelancer. I've been lucky enough that once we work together, we work together again. I've gone all over the world with some of these brands. I basically play the music that you dance to in your underpants when you are getting ready to go out.

I am having so much fun doing this. It's been six years, and I realized what's made me so happy is that I tapped into what made me feel like a teenager again. It reminds me of some motivational speech where I typically would roll my eyes. But now I'm like, "That's me!" I'm that person that I made fun of, and I am having the time of my life.

GET PAID TO
TALK
SPORTS

STEVE GORMAN

FROM

▸

PROFESSIONAL DRUMMER

TO

▸

SPORTS RADIO HOST

IN THE FOURTH GRADE I played in the Hopkinsville, Kentucky, middle school band for about a month until I got kicked out because I refused to practice. I envisioned a concert with adoring fans, but then I had to do marching band music, which was not what I was interested in.

I grew up listening to records and wishing I could be a drummer. My family never had any extra money to say, "Here's a drum kit." I never saved money to buy one. To me, getting a drum kit and starting a band was just a pipe dream. I didn't see a path.

Music and sports, those were my two things. I decided I was going to be a sportscaster and went to college as a broadcasting major. When

I was in college, I met a kid with a drum kit. That was the first time I sat down and played, and right away I could play. I wasn't good, but I knew I could figure it out, and I had a feel for it.

I kind of taught myself. I had been watching drummers my entire life, and looking back now I realize it was pretty obsessively. I was very aware of what the drums should do in a good song. I would focus on how a drummer would lift a part of a song to another place.

My brother was in school at the same time, and I played a New Year's Eve party my freshman year of college with his band. I was decent enough where I could fake it pretty well, and my brother faked it as the singer. We learned twelve songs and played them all three times each for this party. That was the extent of my college drumming.

My senior year of college a friend called and said, "Hey, I'm going to go home and start a band. If you're still playing drums, why don't you just move to Atlanta and do this with me?" I said yes. It was that simple.

I told my friend I was playing a lot more than I actually played, so he just assumed I knew what I was doing. When I got to Atlanta, I walked into a music store and said, "I don't even know what I need. I'm in a band already, and I've never owned a drum kit." I might as well have put the word "sucker" on my forehead. He said, "What's your budget?" And I said, "Seven hundred bucks." I spent $699.99 that day.

At that level especially, on a local music scene when you're trying to write original music and be a new band, it's really all about damage control. No one's good at first. The question is who's the least bad. My greatest strength was that I just was the least bad. Because I had not spent years in my basement practicing drum solos, I wasn't trying to be the star, I wasn't trying to be flashy. I was literally just trying to make it through the song. My head space was *As soon as they realize I don't know what I'm doing, they'll probably replace me, so I'm gonna just not screw this up for as long as I can.*

My roommate in Atlanta was Chris Robinson, who had a band

called Mr. Crowe's Garden. A record label liked one of their demos, but their drummer quit, so Chris asked me to help. I said, "I can't go play a session for A&M Records. I've never been inside a studio before." Chris said, "It's fine. It's a real straight song. You gotta get in there eventually."

This is one of those things I still look back on and think was the craziest thing ever, because I know musicians who spent twelve years hoping a label would give them $5,000 for a demo. I just walked into this thing blind, but the kind of music they were doing fit my playing more than the band I had started with. While we were there, Chris said, "Why don't you just play with us?" And I said, "Yeah, that probably makes sense. Let me think about it." I was torn, because I'd moved to Atlanta to be in the other band.

We started playing in the summer of 1987 and changed our name to the Black Crowes in the summer of 1989. Our first album came out in February 1990. We have played off and on for almost twenty-five years.

In 2001, we broke up the first time, and my wife and I decided to move to LA. I worked on developing a TV show based on the music industry. I ended up getting a production deal with FX, and then FX just blew up and fired everybody and we were back to square one. I was blown away by how slowly things went in TV. People would say, "Yeah, sometimes it'll take ten years to place something."

We moved to Nashville three years later; we wanted to be near friends and family and raise our kids. Surprisingly, the Black Crowes re-formed in 2005, and then I was back in a full-time touring band again. When I got home in 2007, my daughter was in preschool and one of the dads, Willy Daunic, was on a local sports talk station. Every day at the pickup line we would be like, "Hey, did you see the game last night? What did you think?"

One day Willy asked me to come on his show. So I sat in with him for an hour, and we talked about football and the Black Crowes. The program director told me I sounded really good. He asked if I could be a weekly guest. I told him I wanted my own show and that if I could do anything I would have a show with musicians talking sports. It was an idea I'd had in the back of my head for a long time. Because it was Nashville, he liked it.

At the time I remember thinking *It would be great if this turns into something, because I will need a job again one day.* The Black Crowes was a really combustible group. When you start a band with two brothers you are asking for a lot of headaches, and they fought every day of their lives that I've ever known them. The band was always on the verge of breaking up.

Two weeks later, the radio station gave me a shot. The second my producer pointed at me and said "Go," I just thought, *What have I gotten myself into?* The difference between sitting in on someone's show and having your own show is major. I was so out of my depth. I somehow got through it and I kept at it. I had friends cohost with me, and then we were off and running. I did Sunday nights off and on for four years around my touring schedule.

In 2011, I joined a new sports radio station in town, 102.5 The Game. I did the 10-p.m.-to-12-a.m. slot after my kids were in bed. It didn't have a big signal, but the people who found the show were really into it. In 2013, I went on tour and then did my radio show remotely from whatever town I was in. NBC did a piece on me; Clear Channel saw it and reached out under Fox Sports Radio. They liked my show because it is really different. A few months later, in January 2014, they put me on weekends for 230 stations. That was when I thought, *I guess this is what I do right now.* Now I'm on the radio five evenings a week.

When I was in college, I read this quote that said, "Life rewards action." I thought I would get it as a tattoo, but I don't really need to. I have kind of lived by that. I was doing a lot of thinking and planning for both careers before I really realized it. So when they hit, I was ready. Sometimes you have to jump in and see what happens. It's worked so far.

FACE DOWN
IMPOSTER SYNDROME

One of the most surprising things about writing this book has been seeing how many people have experienced imposter syndrome— the feeling that they aren't up to the task. Libby Nelson, the founder and principal of Libby Nelson Coaching, shares her insights into why it happens and five ways you can move on.

REMEMBER THAT YOU'RE NOT THE ONLY ONE

Imposter syndrome is a really universal feeling. I have talked to people at the highest levels of management, and it is something that affects everyone. Pretty much everyone who has been employed has felt that somehow they aren't qualified to be there. Knowing that imposter syndrome isn't unique to you helps you move on.

BLAME YOUR PITCH

In interview or pitch settings, you naturally put only the best part of yourself forward. After you get the job, it is normal to think, *Wow, I kind of fooled them*, which leads to the stress of *Now I have to live up to the hype*.

③

LET GO OF PERFECTION

In our culture, there is such value placed on being an expert. However, creativity and innovation come from not knowing how something will work out—requiring us to ask questions, be vulnerable, try something new. When you realize that true success can come from that place of vulnerability, you put less pressure on yourself to play that part.

④

KEEP LEARNING

I had a client who was so uncomfortable asking questions for fear of appearing like she wasn't an expert that she missed learning information that was crucial to her career. When you stop pretending to have all the answers, you expand your learning and your possibilities for career growth. The most progressive and astute companies value (and expect) curiosity!

⑤

GET SUPPORT

It is really important to have a small circle of professional friends to bounce things off of and talk honestly with about career issues you are facing. Sharing those things with other people who may be experiencing or have already gone through similar issues is incredibly helpful toward feeling more confident and banishing imposter syndrome.

SCREW UP, GET SMARTER,
MOVE UP
IN YOUR CAREER

JASON CARDEN

FROM

HOTEL FRONT
DESK AGENT

TO

PRODUCTION
COMPANY VP OF
DEVELOPMENT

MY PARENTS DIDN'T WANT me to be risk averse, so they would say, "If you make a mistake, you're not going to get in trouble. You're going to get in trouble if you make the same mistake twice." Looking back, I realize that philosophy has helped me navigate my whole career.

I was a performing arts major, and I moved to LA straight out of college, ready to act. I'm from a small town in Virginia, and I didn't know anyone in Hollywood. I slept in my car for a few days, then moved to the couch of a friend of a friend. To pay the bills while I auditioned, I got a job as the front desk agent at the Beverly Hills

Plaza Hotel. It was supposed to be temporary, until I became a working actor.

It turned out the hotel thing was a good fit. In customer service, things go wrong every single day, so putting out fires is your whole job. In dealing with a problem, I wouldn't try to cover it up or make an excuse for it. My approach was always to say, "I understand what you mean. This is bad!" Then I would try to get creative about how to fix it. What I noticed is that if something went wrong and I solved a problem, people would remember and often book another trip because they felt taken care of. If everything is going well, nobody pays attention, but if something misfires and then is corrected, well, now you've done something great. I started to adopt this philosophy that it is actually good when things go wrong, because then you have the opportunity to be a resource for others and hopefully do some good.

I kept moving up and around to different hotels as a bellman, concierge, and ultimately the front desk manager at Shutters on the Beach in Santa Monica. The hotel thing grew because I was making money, and it was something that I excelled at to a certain extent. Five years later, I still wanted that creative outlet, and I was kind of beating myself up because I was not doing what I'd set out to do. It was one of those things where it was like, *What's more important? Is it more important to make money, or is it more important to feel like I'm doing something I should be doing every day and act?*

I had some money saved up, and I quit with the idea that I had to get serious about the acting thing and figure out how to do that in a real way. A few days later, I got a call from my friend who was writing this play based on a conversation we'd had, and he wanted me to act in it. I went to San Francisco to do it. I met my wife, D'Arcy Carden, in the play, so for my personal life it was a good move, too.

It didn't take long before I realized I needed a day job. The play was great, but it wasn't a way to survive. I wanted something where I was making money, but that aligned with acting, so I thought about producing. I figured I could create projects for myself or friends, get paid, and kind of straddle both things. As I got further along, I started to realize that there were better actors than me for certain parts. So then the acting thing slowly ebbed away.

I got in the door by getting any job in a production company that I could get: receptionist or production assistant. It was getting coffee, keeping schedules, answering phones. I did every job that was offered just to get the experience and meet more people. I asked questions of anyone who would talk to me and learned that way. I realized that producing satisfies the creative side and the other skill set that I honed in hotels as a manager.

I gravitated toward comedy and worked as a freelance coordinator for *Saturday Night Live* and as producer and then executive producer for Funny or Die. At both of those places, we were creating a ton of content. At Funny or Die, we were doing between twenty and twenty-five sketches a month. The good thing about that volume is that you don't get precious about things, you hone your instinct for what works because you screw things up a lot.

Right now, I'm vice president of development at Sethmaker Shoemeyers Productions, developing television shows for network, cable, and streaming platforms. Being a good producer effectively means dealing with every kind of problem you can imagine and impossible deadlines, all while guiding the creative and trying to get strong personalities to work collaboratively. This whole philosophy that I've had, that it is okay to fail because then you figure out how to do the next thing, has helped me keep moving forward in my career. The whole mind-set of it is, it's okay to be uncomfortable, it's okay to be a little bit scared, that's a good place to be. You just try not to make the same mistake twice.

SAY GOOD-BYE TO
CORPORATE LIFE

CAROLYN WATERS

FROM — ▸

DIRECTOR
OF CLIENT
MANAGEMENT
AT A FINANCIAL
SERVICES FIRM

▸ **TO** —

LIBRARIAN

> *"While volunteering, I realized what I was missing in my old job: people supporting each other and working as a team."*

MANY PEOPLE WANT TO switch careers, but they can't figure out what else they could possibly do. They worry about taking a financial hit, starting from the ground up, or making a change and having it be worse than their current position. So they stay put for years and years, hoping a viable plan of escape, a genius business idea, or a newly discovered talent or passion will come to them out of the blue. They are waiting for their *That's what I am supposed to be doing* moment.

Though the clear sign from the universe strikes some, for many people it doesn't. So they just keep going and try to ignore those nagging thoughts telling them there is something much better out there.

Take Carolyn Waters. She worked in financial services for twenty years, starting in management consulting and then becoming the director of client management for Mellon Investor Services. For years she thought about doing something else, but it was easier to rise through the ranks than figure out another career path. "When you are good at your job and people recognize that and they keep offering you promotions and more money, it makes it harder and harder to disengage," she says. "You're already in so deep when you've been building your career for twenty years, it seems very risky to let it all go."

As a consultant, Carolyn would be assigned overseas for five weeks at a time, returning for three days, then back onto a plane. There was little time to spend with her husband, much less her friends. An avid book lover, she also never had time to read anything other than work-related items. "When work becomes one hundred percent of your life and you have very little time to do anything else, it isn't healthy," she says.

The cliché career advice is "Do what you love," but Carolyn wasn't sure what that meant, and her twelve- to fourteen-hour workdays didn't leave her with the mental energy to try to figure it out. She decided to approach the problem as if she were solving one for a client. She hatched a plan to leave her job, hoping that time away from deadlines and commitments would lead her in a different direction. "It was the only thing I could think of," she says. "Otherwise I knew I would continue there for the next twenty years."

Figuring out her financial situation was an important consideration. She assessed how much of her savings she could use and how long she and her husband could realistically go without her salary. She knew it would require making some sacrifices and her husband signing on since the belt-tightening would involve him as well. She settled on a six-month sabbatical from work because that time frame also gave her the opportunity to go back to her old life if her break turned out to be fruitless. "I didn't want to take so much time off that my career contacts wouldn't want to take me back or take another chance on me."

To make sure that her work reputation didn't take a hit, Carolyn did not give a reason for quitting. When rumors swirled, she had to confirm that she wasn't ill and she wasn't accepting her former boss's offer to become COO of his new start-up. However, she still didn't divulge what she was doing.

During her time off, Carolyn spent a lot of time doing all the things she'd never had time for: visiting museums, spending time with friends, reading, taking long walks, and volunteering. "I began going to the Mid-Manhattan Branch of the New York Public Library to check out books to read and to use it as a place to work and think about what my future life would look like," she says. "I thought volunteering there seemed like a good use of my new free time. I'd be able to spend more time at a place I loved, help out a great organization, and observe a completely new kind of work environment."

As a volunteer, Carolyn worked one or two days a week. It didn't take long for her to want to be much more involved. "As a former management consultant, I had lots of ideas about how to fix things I saw that weren't working. The librarians encouraged me to discuss my thoughts with the head of the branch, and he even implemented some of my recommendations," she says. "That's when I knew librarianship was for me. That culture of support and being open to new ideas was so refreshing. I realized what I was missing in my old job: people supporting each other and working as a team. Plus, they all shared my love of books."

With the encouragement of the librarians she worked with, Carolyn applied for her master's in library science at Pratt Institute School of Information. As fate would have it, the day she received her acceptance to the program was exactly six months after she took time off to start on her six-month quest.

A decade later, Carolyn is the head librarian at the New York Society Library. Would she ever consider shifting gears again? Surrounded by books, passionate readers, and supportive colleagues, Carolyn is emphatic that she's in the right place. "I'm never leaving!"

CREATE A
FINANCIAL SAFETY NET

Ditching your monotonous job in favor of something that feels more rewarding sounds amazing in theory, but you need to prepare for the financial reality of a job change. How much of a cushion will you need if you want to start your own business or take on a job where you will be making less than you are used to? Two financial advisers, Debra Schatzki, the founder of BPP Wealth Solutions, and Mark J. McCooey, a financial adviser at Morgan Stanley, have advised dozens of clients on how to switch careers. Here are each of their top three suggestions for anyone ready to make a change.

MARK'S ADVICE

1
PLAN IN ADVANCE

Make the decision to try something new when you want to—don't let a business, job, or industry die around you and dictate when you have to make a change. If you want to make a move, start planning now.

2
HAVE A REALISTIC AMOUNT OF MONEY ON HAND

Really think about what you want to do and how much money you will need in the bank to survive over several years, not just one. Regardless of whether you are going to try to be a financial adviser, real estate agent, consultant, or painter, it may take anywhere from two to five years to really build your business and stem the flow of cash out, so that is how much money you need in the bank.

DON'T WASTE MONEY

When you are thinking about cutting back on expenses, focus on the little things, because they really add up. Avoid Starbucks (make your own coffee), cut out overpriced fast-casual lunches (pack your own), and get rid of your monthly gym membership (run outside for free). Cancel subscriptions that you don't use, and let all that spare cash add up in your bank account.

DEBRA'S ADVICE

BE WILLING TO CHANGE YOUR LIFESTYLE

You may not be able to have the same lifestyle as before, so you should see what changes will result in less overhead. Changes such as moving to a smaller place or even moving to a different part of the country, town, or neighborhood can drastically lower your cost of living. It's all about what is important to you. If pursuing your passion is the goal, you will have to adjust everything to make it a reality.

CONSULT A FINANCIAL ADVISER

Your financial decisions should all be customized to what your goals are, what your expenses are, and what your income is. A financial adviser will help you make a strong financial plan and prepare.

KNOW THAT HAVING A GOAL WILL HELP YOU RESET

When people are excited to achieve a certain goal, whether it be retiring, going back to school, or making a career move, they immediately start approaching spending differently. When you realize your dream life is attainable if you make changes, that is an excellent motivation.

WORK WITH YOUR
HANDS

ERIC GORGES

FROM

ACCOUNT MANAGER

TO

MOTORCYCLE
BUILDER, TV HOST

WHEN I WAS 26, I had my first panic attack. I was scuba diving on vacation, about eighty feet underwater, when I started to breathe fast and shallow. A wave of heat came over my body. It was terrifying. I managed to grab a line attached to the boat and pulled myself up. By the time I got to twenty feet, I was able to calm down enough to hang out there for a few minutes. When I got out, I had no idea what had happened. I didn't even know what a panic attack was.

When I got home, everything seemed back to normal. I went back to my job working in IT at Xerox in metro Detroit, where I had been since starting as a stock boy at 16. I was always a tech nerd, from the time I was 8, so when Xerox was transforming from an analog company to digital, I was a computer geek in the right place at the right time.

I liked my job; it was challenging. Over the years, I moved through the ranks, eventually becoming an account manager. In my free time, I rode motorcycles and did mechanical work on my own bikes and friends' bikes.

A few months after that first panic attack, I had another one. From then on they started to happen pretty regularly. I had one on a plane, and I didn't want to fly again. I started to have these different symptoms: chest pains, anxiousness, nervousness. I couldn't figure out what was going on. I was in test after test. I literally thought I was going crazy. I thought I was going to die of a heart attack. I was having six to eight panic attacks a day, every day. It was not a fun time in my life. It was an embarrassment to me. It kept getting worse. After a few months, I became agoraphobic. I couldn't leave my house. I couldn't make it to work.

I began seeing a shrink. One day he asked, "If money and knowledge and training didn't matter, what would you want to do?" I thought about how I had been fascinated with bikes from the time I was young, and I happened to be rebuilding a motorcycle in my garage at the time. I immediately said, "I would work with my hands, either woodworking, which is what my grandfather did, or building motorcycles." So his advice was to figure out how to do one of those things. I thought, *Seriously? That will get rid of my problems?* He could have told me to go to Mars, and I would have done it.

I didn't waste a lot of time. I reached out to a local metal fabricator, Ron Fournier. I had met Ron at his shop and stopped in there regularly. He offered me an apprenticeship, and I left Xerox.

Ron taught me everything about metalship and welding. I was getting paid $8 an hour. After a few months, the job that they had hired me for didn't come through, so they couldn't keep me. I said, "I just want to learn, you don't have to pay me." I knew I was getting paid in knowledge. He told me that in turn I could use his equipment to work on my own stuff and sell projects. It was tough financially. I was married at the time. We were living off of my wife's income for a few years.

I began by selling handmade items like fenders, tanks, and handlebars. I cold-called and drove out to shops to let them know I hand built and modified bikes and ask them if they needed anything. One guy said yes. That was the start. I founded Voodoo Choppers in 1999.

It wasn't a situation where my panic attacks went away after my job change. They diminished over time. I was lucky in that regard; for some people their world shrinks and continues to shrink. For me, my world was shrinking fast, but eventually it started to grow again. It took time. But the majority of my being the way that I am I attribute to what I do for a living and how I work. Working with my hands and being able to lose myself in time while creating something really helped me. There is an amazing transformation that happens when you work with your hands. I now host a show on PBS called *A Craftsman's Legacy*, featuring craftspeople around the country.

The definition of success is different for everybody. To me success means I have a roof over my head, I can pay my bills and hopefully find more business. I have been to a point where I couldn't afford to eat and had the repo man around, but you make things work, you keep moving forward. Anybody can run a business. It is really about persistence. Sometimes you don't want to keep pushing forward; eventually you realize that's the only way you'll make it through.

GO FOR FINANCIAL INDEPENDENCE

NANCY COOLEY

FROM

—

FOOD STORE
OWNER

TO

—

PRIVATE WEALTH
ADVISER

T HE IDEA THAT YOU should know what you want to do professionally when you graduate is not realistic. Your twenties can be tumultuous—you are moving, trying different jobs, different relationships. Eventually, after a lot of varied experiences, this disorderly path begins to take shape and forms a foundation for what you are going to do later in life.

I grew up in northern California, one of four children, with parents who entertained often. As a child, I would sit in the kitchen with the caterers and soon developed a love for food and the community that it represented. I went on to work for the catering company in high school and college, which led to my pursuing a job in the food world.

After college, I moved to New York City and landed a job at Dean & DeLuca. I was given the opportunity to work in the pastry department with the promise of being sponsored to go to John Clancy's baking school. Under the watchful eye of owners Joel Dean and Giorgio DeLuca, they came to trust that I understood what they were looking for—quality of the product was paramount, presentation equally so, and of course taste. I became the de facto head of the pastry department.

The following summer I spent weekends on Fire Island. A lease on a hardware store became available, and some friends and I decided that we should open our own specialty food store. We naively thought we could have a summer business that would afford us the ability to pursue our more focused passions during the year.

My father cosigned a loan from a bank for $16,000 to convert the space and buy the equipment we needed. None of us knew anything about starting a business and even less about running one. It was challenging. While the store was very well received, we quickly realized that we would have to work through the winter to make our loan payments.

In the end, I never went back to Dean & DeLuca and never went to baking school. We kept the store open for seven years, including two long winters when we were the only store open on the entire island. That made it necessary to transition from selling gourmet foods and no meat to making bacon, egg, and cheese breakfast sandwiches, whatever would sell, so that we could make our payments. Our hard work paid off, and the store became a successful business.

Ultimately, my partners and I decided that we wanted to pursue other interests, so we didn't renew the lease. I followed my heart to Vermont to live with my boyfriend. I took what started out as a part-time job at a clothing store to support myself. A number of months into that new job, the owner ended up with a serious back injury, and once again I found myself working at something that I had never done before: managing a retail boutique, which included buying, selling, and merchandising.

Several years later, I returned to California—heartbroken. At the ripe old age of 28, I had decided that life wasn't going to come with a man on a permanent basis. So my number one priority was to make enough money to be self-supporting and have the things I wanted: a house, a family, financial security. If I wasn't going to be someone's wife, I'd have to do it myself.

I went to a talk by an author who had just written a book about sales careers for women. One of the opportunities she discussed was becoming a stockbroker. I was shocked that one didn't need to have an MBA (which I didn't have) to be a financial adviser. If you are hired, the best-established firms offer a strong training program, and if you are successful, there is unlimited income potential. I reasoned that if I didn't succeed, at least I would gain a fundamental understanding of investments and finance and acquire skills that I knew would be meaningful and important to me in my life.

I launched a campaign to learn all that I could about investment banking and the financial services industry. In a matter of weeks, I went from knowing no stockbrokers to knowing a few dozen. A handful of them agreed to meet me, which led to interviews with a number of firms. One of those firms was Drexel Burnham Lambert. I managed to make

> "
> *My*
> NUMBER
> ONE PRIORITY
> *was to make*
> *enough money to be*
> SELF-SUPPORTING.

it to the last round of interviews—it was me and a young man named Reid. Drexel called me to say, "We just want to let you know that we decided to hire Reid." I said, "You're making a big mistake. It's not that you shouldn't hire Reid, you should hire both of us." We were both hired.

Though the industry was (and still is) male dominated, I was razor focused on my clients and highly motivated to tackle this new challenge and to show my firm that they had not made a mistake. Over time, I transitioned to an advisory practice offering investment management consulting along with a full range of wealth management solutions.

I really enjoy working with individuals and the difference I make in their lives. It is immensely rewarding to help people achieve their financial and life goals. In the end, I also attained my own goal of financial independence and managed to have a family, too, as the business and my firm gave me the flexibility to achieve work-life balance. The sky's the limit—a career shouldn't upend one's personal life, and one's personal life shouldn't upend a career.

LEAVE
YOUR JOB,
THEN GO BACK

ROBERT HAMMOND

FROM	TO	SIDE GIG
COFOUNDER AND EXECUTIVE DIRECTOR OF A NONPROFIT PUBLIC SPACE IN NYC	COFOUNDER AND EXECUTIVE DIRECTOR OF A NONPROFIT PUBLIC SPACE IN NYC	VEDIC MEDITATION INSTRUCTOR

> *"I always felt that for happiness, I had to keep moving or doing something new. . . . But what was so interesting was that by coming back, I found it's the best place."*

IN 1999, ROBERT HAMMOND read a *New York Times* article discussing the possible demolition of the abandoned elevated railway that ran through his downtown Manhattan neighborhood. He attended a local community board meeting with the idea that the space should be saved and converted into something new. There he met Joshua David, and the two eventually came up with a proposal to turn the High Line into a park.

Saving the High Line seemed like the type of idea that is so brilliant you want it to happen but has so many things going against it that it is impossible. Thanks to Robert and Josh's relentless determination, the High Line has been open for almost ten years. A magical place that pairs wild with urban, community with solitude, it has completely changed the dynamic of Manhattan's far West Side.

The success of the High Line made Robert a rock star in the world of preservation and city planning. However, the myth that he ditched a desk job to save the High Line has followed him around as well. "There is a lot of romance in this idea of just leaving your job and doing something new and big," he says. "I talk to a lot of people doing start-ups and civic projects. They're so risky and take so long. I always urge people to have another job, too. I didn't quit my corporate job and start working full-time for the High Line. It took four years." After founding Friends of the High Line, Robert worked on the preservation project while simultaneously working at an internet start-up and running an in-flight catalog business.

As passionate as Robert was about turning the High Line from concept to thriving park, he never planned on having it become his full-time job. "I wanted someone else to take it on, someone who had experience, because we didn't have any experience doing this kind of thing," he admits. "When we realized no one else was going to do it, we just got started."

Robert stayed at the High Line for fourteen years, seeing it through the opening of sections one and two. At each stage, there were new challenges to deal with, and clearing those obstacles kept him invested in staying. However, he always wondered about other paths, other roads not taken, and what would be his next act, but he was so focused on the day-to-day, he knew that he needed to leave to figure out what that would be. In 2013, he saw an opportunity for a graceful exit. "We opened section two, we raised enough money for section three, and it was secured that the High Line wasn't going to be demolished. I decided it was a good time for me to go."

After Robert announced his departure, there was a fawning piece in the *New York Times*. There were good-bye parties. He said farewell and decided to spend his first three months post–High Line in India learning to teach meditation. He discovered the practice seven years prior and credits it for making him feel generally happier and more Zen. "I initially tried meditation when I was in my twenties because I had anxiety and I couldn't sleep. I tried classes, tapes, and seminars, and I couldn't stick with any of them. But I kept trying," he recalls. "I started doing Vedic meditation, and it just clicked. I was able to keep doing it. It just made this huge difference for me. I felt like it changed my life."

After Robert learned to meditate, he encouraged his friends to learn as well. He had so many friends who benefited from meditation that he wanted to teach. After he returned from India, he taught full-time while interviewing for a variety of jobs. "Working at the High Line, you don't actually see results for a long time. When I teach meditation, I see the results in people after four days. It's incredible."

Then, in 2014, out of the blue the High Line called. They wanted him back. "I said no. I was just starting to work on some new projects that I was interested in. I was enjoying teaching. The idea of going back also felt a little embarrassing. I had left in a very public way," Robert explains. "It just felt like going backward."

Robert eventually agreed to go back temporarily as the interim executive director with the condition that the board hire a headhunter and start a search. "There was a whole new set of issues, the problem of being too popular or that the neighborhood had become such a catalyst for economic development," Robert says. "Now we are focusing on, What are we going to be when we grow up? How do we create a new cultural institution for the twenty-first century? It feels exciting."

Within a few months, Robert found himself falling in love with his old job all over again. He also found himself wanting to stay. "It was a really hard decision for me because it didn't really make a lot of sense. For me, it made more sense to leave, to do something new," he says. "I always felt that for happiness, I had to keep moving or doing something new. I felt like staying at this job that I had already done for fifteen years, that was not where I was going to find contentment. But what was so interesting was that by coming back, I found it's the best place; I'm enjoying my job more now than I ever enjoyed it before." He still teaches meditation on the side and feels that the growth that has come from the practice also helped him see his role at the High Line with fresh eyes. "I think I had to leave. Leaving was really critical for the process."

"

THIS WHOLE PHILOSOPHY THAT I'VE HAD, THAT IT IS OKAY TO FAIL BECAUSE THEN YOU FIGURE OUT HOW TO DO THE NEXT THING, HAS HELPED ME KEEP MOVING FORWARD IN MY CAREER. THE WHOLE MIND-SET OF IT IS, IT'S OKAY TO BE UNCOMFORTABLE, IT'S OKAY TO BE A LITTLE BIT SCARED, THAT'S A GOOD PLACE TO BE. YOU JUST TRY NOT TO MAKE THE SAME MISTAKE TWICE.

JASON CARDEN

"Move Up in Your Career," page 181

6

BECOME A WELLNESS WARRIOR

Run Toward a Better Life / Choose Two Careers Instead of One / Launch a Brand in Your Kitchen / Go Back to Work After a Parenting Gap / Blog Your Way to a New Business

IT'S ALL ABOUT TRANSFORMATION. When you are obsessed with health and fitness, it is because you see the impact.

Maybe you started because you wanted to lose weight or clear your skin. Perhaps you needed to find an outlet for energy that was manifesting into something negative rather than positive. Maybe you just needed something to feel good about. Whatever it was that got you to change your perception, you now see food as fuel, and fitness as a route to confidence, Zen, and happiness. Now you're hooked.

Once you've seen the power of wellness to reboot, you want to take what you've learned and keep going, whether it means teaching or inspiring others or continuing to up your personal goals. There are so many different paths to take and ways to get there. The people in this chapter have used health and fitness to live their best lives as athletes, teachers, app developers, cooks, bloggers, dancers, and entrepreneurs. They had the courage to follow a different path. Now it's your turn.

RUN
TOWARD A
BETTER LIFE

MAGGIE GUTERL

FROM
—
BARTENDER

TO
—
**MARKETING
SPECIALIST AND
ULTRAMARATHONER**

*"I remember the exact moment I realized
that I loved running. . . . It was mile seven
[of a ten-mile race]. People were cheering, I had
music playing, and I just thought,
Why have I not been doing this all along?"*

WHEN MAGGIE GUTERL WAS a New York City bartender in her twenties, she usually got home just as the sun was rising. Exercise? That rarely happened. Sleep? That took place during the day. Today Maggie is a competitive runner who has completed more than fifty-six ultramarathons and thirty marathons. She now starts her day at 5 a.m. to get in her training before work. The stark contrast between her life before running and after is not lost on her. "That was a crazy period in my life. It affects you mentally, never seeing daylight," she says. "Now I crave it."

In her mid-twenties, Maggie moved to Philadelphia, hoping to leave the nocturnal life behind. "There was a whole downward spiral and chain of events. Eventually, I knew I needed to do something with my life now that I didn't have the one hobby I had spent so much time doing, which was drinking and going to bars," she reveals. "I wanted a change and felt like running could be that for me."

Maggie's pivot into fitness began with a New Year's resolution to get healthy and run a ten-mile race. For someone who had never taken exercise seriously, running seemed like an easy place to start, and she took to it instantly. That May she ran the Broad Street ten-mile run. The experience was exhilarating. "I remember the exact moment I realized that I loved running and that I had found that thing. It was mile seven, and I was turning the corner around City Hall. People were cheering, I had music playing, and I just thought, *This is awesome! Why have I not been doing this all along?*" She found herself drawn to the solitude and calm of training runs, the camaraderie of races, and the high that comes from setting goals and ripping past them.

After marathons became her norm, Maggie tried ultramarathons, which vary in distance but usually start at 30 miles. Her first one involved running for twenty-four hours, but it was a challenge. "I didn't know anything about nutrition. I was projectile vomiting soda," she recalls. Her goal was to run 100 miles; she ran an impressive 97.

However, Maggie wasn't satisfied, so the following year, fueled by healthy food, she came back and ran 110 miles in twenty-four hours.

In 2013, Maggie had a goal of qualifying for the United States 24 Hour National Team and worked with coach Michele Yates on fitness and nutrition. "I told her I wanted to run over 136 miles in twenty-four hours and get on the team. She didn't doubt me once." Eventually she ran 142 miles to qualify, and in 2015 she went to Italy for the World Championships, where she ran 146 miles and came in fourth individually and the team won gold.

Maggie currently trains 50 to 100 miles a week around her full-time job as the marketing coordinator at Nathan Sports, a company that makes running gear. "A lot of the top elite athletes have other jobs," she explains. "It's not easy. Could I be a much better runner if I didn't have a full-time job and could focus on training and recovery day in and day out? Probably. But no one does this sport for the money. I could name a tiny handful of mostly male athletes who are getting compensated enough to not do anything else besides ultrarunning. Even then, most of them do some kind of trail camps or coaching—or just live out of their cars."

Despite her intense schedule, running energizes Maggie rather than exhausting her. "I feel super tired and terrible when I don't run," she explains. The only downside is the cost of traveling. In order to compete, travel is crucial, but it adds up and most races hand out trophies rather than cash as compensation.

Looking back on her life before running, Maggie is happy she made the choice to make it her focus. "My life has done a one-eighty," she says. "It sounds cliché but my biggest hurdle was the mental one. I probably had the running ability in me—untapped—for a long time."

TRANSFORM LIVES
ONE CLIMB
AT A TIME

STACY BARE

FROM

US ARMY
CAPTAIN

TO

ADVOCATE FOR
VETERANS AND THE
HEALING POWER
OF NATURE

"For some people it may be fly fishing or gardening or hunting or climbing or skiing, but there is power in the outdoors."

THE FIRST TIME STACY Bare went climbing, he was in a dark place. The US Army veteran returned from Iraq in 2007, and three years later he still felt untethered. He describes the feeling as "Where do I go from here? What is my identity now that I'm not in the army?" He was battling with post-traumatic stress disorder (PTSD), feeling guilty that he wasn't in battle supporting his friends and overwhelmed by the idea that he had survived when others hadn't. The trauma he experienced was emerging in toxic ways, and he was battling thoughts of ending his life as well as developing a severe alcohol and drug addiction.

Stacy shared his pain with a close friend, who invited him to a popular climbing site, Flatirons, near Boulder, Colorado. "Innately I think he knew it would be healing," Stacy says. "He thought it was something I needed to do—find another reason to live and something to look forward to." During that first climb, Stacy felt fueled by being immersed in the moment and concentrating only on his next move. When he arrived at the top, proud that he had accomplished the task at hand, exhilarated and exhausted, he experienced a sort of traumatic release. "My whole body was shaking," he says. "All the years of trying to contain the trauma, the anger, the fear, it all just came out." Once that subsided, he felt a clarity he hadn't felt before. "I didn't feel guilty about living anymore. I didn't feel fearful about what the future would bring."

That experience propelled Stacy toward healing, deeper friendships, and understanding the powerful link among the outdoors, fitness, and mental health. He wanted to keep climbing, to keep living, and for the first time in many years he felt optimism and a vision for something larger. "I thought, *Man, we need to get more people out climbing and definitely more veterans out climbing*," he says. "For some people it may be fly fishing or gardening or hunting or climbing or skiing, but there is power in the outdoors."

Along with fellow army veteran Nick Watson, Stacy founded Veterans Expeditions, a Colorado-based nonprofit dedicated to getting veterans into outdoor programs. "At the time, nobody was really doing anything like this. We opened up another avenue and channel for people to connect with the physical country they served, find the benefit of time outdoors, and move forward with their lives."

Stacy moved on to become the director of Sierra Club Outdoors for seven years. There, he oversaw programs to connect 265,000 people annually to the outdoors through youth, military, and community activities. Currently, Stacy is working on two long-term projects to help veterans. He is continuing his work with the Great Outdoors Lab, which he founded in partnership with Dr. Dacher Keltner at the Greater Good Science Center at UC Berkeley. The goal is to put scientific data behind the idea of outdoor adventure as an alternative form of health care that can result in less dependence on medication and lower health care costs. Stacy is also returning with other veterans to the places they only experienced in war. His goal is to rewrite the narrative by forming meaningful connections with the people in each country and exploring the landscape—for example, climbing in Angola and skiing in Iraq. A short documentary on Adventure Not War premiered at the Tribeca Film Festival in 2018.

Stacy's devotion to helping others out of dark places has had powerful consequences in his own life. "I've been home for ten-plus years, and I've spent a lot of time and energy working to get better," he says. "I still struggle, but I spend time outdoors. I seek help. I think you can get to a point where you really move forward."

Part of moving forward has been creating a family; he's now married with a 2-year-old daughter. "I'm finding so much joy in all these things I never thought I would be doing. Moving to the suburbs, the privilege of buying a house. Realizing that all of life can be really exciting and beautiful, even though it also can be really boring, routine, and unsexy, and finding joy in that anyway."

Though climbing was first a way of finding solace, Stacy is grateful that he's been able to make empowering others his career. "Seeing service members, veterans, peers, and those in recovery having a similar type of awe-inspiring experience is really something incredible," says Stacy. "It only makes me healthier and stronger and more committed to this work and to expanding this work."

TRANSITION
OUT OF THE
MILITARY

Judson Kauffman spent ten years as a Navy SEAL but struggled to find work afterward. He started a management consulting firm, Exbellum, to help connect military veterans to business careers. Over time, his Austin, Texas–based company has transitioned to leadership coaching and consulting for businesses. Here are his top five transition tips.

KNOW THAT YOUR MILITARY EXPERIENCE IS VALUABLE

I have noticed that veterans consistently perform at or above the level of their civilian peers within the companies they join. That goes for people leaving a military vocational role and wanting to get into a blue-collar job, up to leaders from the military who want to get into business.

BRANCH OUT

You're not limited to staying in security or defense. You just might need to take a few steps back before you start in a fresh career. Maybe you're expecting to make $65,000 a year coming out but the first job offer you get is $40,000 and it's working for someone who's got less experience as a manager than you do. It's okay to take that; it'll pay off in the long run.

3

APPLY TO VETERAN-FRIENDLY CAREERS AND COMPANIES

Blue-collar businesses such as construction companies and resource companies have always loved veterans. The military spends a lot of money investing in the training of various vocational roles for jobs such as welders and mechanics. Many companies like to take advantage of that investment. Since the military can be so demanding on people, service members are also well conditioned for a career in finance. Tech has also learned to appreciate military veterans in a big way. Many tech firms have founding teams whose members are brilliant technologists but have never managed an organization; they need someone to keep the team focused, organized, and moving in a positive direction. The military is an excellent source of this type of operational and management talent. We've seen large companies such as Pinterest and Apple, as well as countless tech start-ups, recruit military veterans for chief of staff– or operations director-type roles.

4

GET JOB-SEEKING SUPPORT

There are many organizations offering support for veterans who are transitioning out. The two we like the most are VETTED and BreakLine. These are both not-for-profit organizations that have some very talented people running them; they combine education with transition support.

5

MARKET YOUR RÉSUMÉ TO CIVILIAN EMPLOYERS

The best advice I have to make your résumé more friendly to civilian jobs is to keep it to one page and to have someone with no military experience help you write it. The skills translator tool at https://www.military.com is very useful when describing your experience on a résumé.

CHOOSE
TWO CAREERS
INSTEAD OF ONE

PAYAL KADAKIA

COFOUNDER AND EXECUTIVE CHAIRMAN OF A CLASS-BOOKING APP	**AND**	FOUNDER AND ARTISTIC DIRECTOR FOR A DANCE COMPANY

LAUNCHING A DANCE COMPANY I fell in love with Indian dance when I was young; it was a way of connecting with my culture and my ancestors. Especially because I was born and raised here in America, it was nice to have that connection. I created a dance troupe at MIT, and after

graduation, I realized there was no professional outlet the way there is for ballet or jazz. I wanted to create a platform of awareness of Indian dance to really share the culture and richness and beauty of India.

RUNNING A BUSINESS Launching Sa Dance Company taught me how to be an entrepreneur. I had to coordinate schedules, rent space for practice, and work on branding and marketing. For our first show, we rented out a small studio space and posted on Facebook, worried that no one would come. I will never forget walking out and seeing 250 people there. Soon after, we rented out the main theater at Alvin Ailey for a day and a half. I had to write a check for $20,000 out of my own pocket. We did three shows and sold 1,000 tickets and I made it all back.

FOUNDING A START-UP I founded Sa in 2008 when I was 25 as a way to keep dance in my life while working at Warner Music Group on digital strategy and business development. During that time, I went out to San Francisco for WMG and met all of these amazing entrepreneurs. I was very inspired to build something great on my own. I gave myself two weeks to come up with an idea and thirty-six hours later came up with the initial concept that eventually turned into ClassPass.

LANDING ON THE RIGHT IDEA When companies succeed, they've found the right product market fit, which means you have a product that customers really want and are willing to pay for. It took us three years to figure out the model and the product. It is really hard to get customers to change their behavior and do something that they weren't doing before. The initial idea was a search engine called Classivity, and a lot of that learning and technology went into building what ClassPass is today, a fitness class membership app with access to more than 8,500 classes around the country.

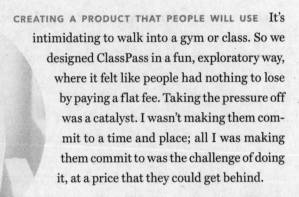

CREATING A PRODUCT THAT PEOPLE WILL USE It's intimidating to walk into a gym or class. So we designed ClassPass in a fun, exploratory way, where it felt like people had nothing to lose by paying a flat fee. Taking the pressure off was a catalyst. I wasn't making them commit to a time and place; all I was making them commit to was the challenge of doing it, at a price that they could get behind.

LEADING BY EXAMPLE I always have my investors come watch Sa perform. I don't think they can understand me without watching me dance. When people watch me or my company perform, you see our passion for dance. That is the same passion and expression that we want to bring out in other people through ClassPass. It's one thing to say we want people to live better; it's another to show them.

NEEDING TO DO BOTH JOBS There have definitely been times it was hard, but every single time I got further away from dance, the mission of ClassPass didn't make sense to me. I had to keep dancing to keep the vision and my customer at the forefront. I dance at least four to five hours a week, ten to twenty when we have a show. It is the perfect break in the day. Dancing helps me think through things that I deal with at ClassPass. That's the beauty of doing both and being creative and analytical at the same time. They actually help each other.

LAUNCH A BRAND IN YOUR
KITCHEN

AGATHA ACHINDU

FROM

IT PROFESSIONAL

TO

FOUNDER OF A
HEALTHY BABY
FOOD COMPANY

> *"If I had given up, I would never have known that this would be the success that it is today."*

IT **WAS THE IMPOSSIBILITY** of keeping up with a demanding job in IT for a Fortune 500 company while simultaneously trying to cook nutritious baby food from scratch that led Agatha Achindu down an entirely different career path. "You shouldn't only eat homemade baby food because your mom or dad stays at home or, because your parents are working, eat baby food that has been sitting on a shelf for three years," says Agatha, who grew up in Cameroon, where farm-to-table was her everyday reality. "My thought was there should be a company doing food that is exactly like parents want to do at home. Not everybody has the know-how or the capacity to make this type of food, but every child should have access to it."

Despite a hectic schedule as a working mom with an infant son, Agatha felt so passionately about all children eating well that she volunteered to teach cooking to new mothers, posting flyers at a local Atlanta-area hospital. "I would cook in my home for free," says Agatha, who taught more than three hundred women. "Even though I was teaching them how to make their own baby food, I realized what people liked was the convenience of having the food made." That's when the idea for Yummy Spoonfuls was born.

To avoid using preservatives and having her products sitting on store shelves for a long time, Agatha came up with an innovative freezing method, putting her products in the freezer aisles. "We make our food the same way you make it at home. It's real ingredients—an apple that is very gently steamed with nothing added, no citric acid, no water, just blended. What is different is that we use a flash freezing system to keep food fresh and nutrients in," she says.

When Agatha decided to launch her idea, her first stop was the Small Business Administration district office in Atlanta, which directed her to a subset of SBA called SCORE, led by retired executives. She was teamed up with a mentor, who suggested she start by writing a business plan. When she was done, she had an outline for how to get started. Those first few years, she and a small team worked out of a shared commercial kitchen in Marietta.

One business move that Agatha regrets is how she funded her venture. "The biggest mistake I made when I launched was not to look for investment at that point. I used all of our kids' savings, our 401(k), everything we owned, I used it. The lesson that I learned is that you borrow money when you have money, because it's easy for somebody to give you money when you have $50K cash in your bank rather than when you don't have a penny." Agatha's biggest piece of advice for other entrepreneurs is to understand finances before you launch. "A lot of small businesses fail, just because of the surprise factor of money."

Luckily, Agatha's husband was supportive of the financial risk and actively involved in getting the enterprise off the ground. "I left a high-paying job to create a start-up. For years I didn't get a salary, because we were just putting money back into the business," she explains. "My husband was doing two or three jobs, and he would come in the kitchen at night and stew twenty-five to fifty pounds of carrots."

In 2008, a woman who had been in Agatha's parenting group introduced her to a relative who worked at Amazon, and the company's sales skyrocketed. "That is when we really started looking for funding. We had a total of five employees. So it was really difficult making everything from scratch by hand. There were days we would cook three days straight, nineteen-hour days, to ship food," Agatha says. "The good thing was we made food to order. I didn't want to sit on capital, I didn't want to be paying for storage. With Amazon, we knew the things that were the top sellers, we made batches and batches of those." Today Agatha's top client is Walmart.

"This is just something that I started from just wanting to help, and today it is a multimillion-dollar company. It hasn't been the easiest journey. But I was able to stick it out, and look at where we are! If I had given up, I would never have known that this would be the success that it is today." Agatha says there were many times she thought about quitting. "The first time that I was really close, I said, 'You know what, God? I know you have a plan, but this is too much work.' The next week we won Best Baby Food in the United States. Every time I feel like giving up, God will just drop something that is enough for me to know that I can hang in there, I got this." Agatha's focus through tough times is on gratitude. "Every time I get an email or someone writes on social media about Yummy Spoonfuls, I look up and say, 'Thank you, Lord, for blessing me.' It is not a job. It is a gift."

GO BACK TO WORK AFTER A PARENTING GAP

Going back to work after a parenting gap can be a challenge, and the longer you're out, the harder it is to get back in. Jennifer Gefsky, after her own seven-year parenting leave from a law career, cofounded Après, a job marketplace for women reentering the workforce. She shares five pieces of advice from how to address your time off to scoring a job offer.

1

YOU HAVE TO *REALLY* WANT TO GO BACK

We'd all like to work part-time, and maybe after a year you can ask about a more flexible schedule, but companies really do that only when employees have established themselves. It is rare to see those jobs for new employees, so know that if you want to go back to work, you have to be all in.

2

YOU MIGHT NEED TO TAKE A STEP BACKWARD

If you were a senior vice president when you left your job, you may not be coming back to that position or salary, especially if you have a gap of several years.

GET YOURSELF UP TO SPEED

You have to educate yourself and keep up with what is going on in the industry. You can't go into an interview and say, "I haven't worked in five or ten years, but here I am, ready to go." You have to establish what you have done to stay on top of your skills and get yourself back up to speed. "I've interned here. I've taken this class . . . " Something that establishes a commitment to what you are doing. Return-to-work internships are a great way to show that commitment.

CONSIDER A CAREER SWITCH

One of the great benefits of taking a career break is that it allows people to step back and think about what they are passionate about. Let's say you were in law and hated it, and now you want to go do X. So when you are interviewing for that X, you can say, "I know this is what I want to do. I studied it, I believe in it, and I am energized about it!" There is a lot to be said for an applicant who is super charged up about working for a company—people love that.

NETWORK, NETWORK, NETWORK

If you have been out of the workforce, the best thing you can do is start networking with anyone and everyone. Contact former colleagues, and reach out to friends and family members. Ask if you can take them for coffee to get their advice. Be strategic in your networking—go into a meeting knowing what your "ask" is going to be, whether that is a reference, a referral to human resources, or a specific job you want to be considered for.

BLOG
YOUR WAY TO A NEW BUSINESS

KEVIN CURRY

FROM → SENIOR COMMUNICATIONS ANALYST

TO → FOOD BLOGGER AND HEALTHY LIFESTYLE EXPERT

IT ALL STARTED WHEN I saw a bad photo of myself on Facebook. I had no neck or jawline. I didn't realize that I had let myself go. So I did what everybody does: tried to out-train a poor diet by running continuously on the treadmill. I worked out three hours a day for about a year, and my body wasn't changing. Food was the thing that was really doing me in.

I tried cookie-cutter meal plans, lots of chicken, broccoli, and brown rice. Then I would eat real food, and the weight was right back on. I just didn't believe that we should be put on this earth with all these amazing cuisines and not be able to eat them. So I bought every book on nutrition that I could find at the half-price bookstore. I figured out how to swap out the ingredients to make dishes I liked healthier. When I did that, the weight just began to fall off. Within about a month my clothes were fitting differently, people were commenting. That helped accelerate my success and motivate me more.

I started a blog on Tumblr called *Fit Men Cook* to share my recipes, build a community, and keep me accountable and on track. I thought people would come in and critique my diet and give me advice, but people started looking to me for advice. One morning I posted a banana split made with yogurt. The photo went viral on social media. People began to share it and copy it and redo the recipe. That was the tipping point—I went from 10,000 to 100,000 followers in about a month.

I created a WordPress site and thought, *Let me just put some ads up there*. Then brands began to ask me to try their products out, and I began to make money. The first year, I made about $25,000. After a couple months of doing that, I thought, *If you're spending about 40 percent of your time doing this and you're making this much money, then how much more could you make if you increased it?*

I went to my boss at Dell, and he gave me some really good advice that gave me the confidence to actually go ahead and go for it. He said, "I would hire you back if you wanted to come back, and in fifteen or twenty years from now, you want to be able to sit your grandkids down on your lap and not say, 'Here's this really cool thing I did called *Fit Men Cook*. Here's how I effed it all up,' but 'Here's how I did it and made it win.'"

When I quit my job, I didn't have that much money saved up. I had $15,000 in the bank, so I gave myself about six months and went for it. The majority of my income comes from sponsorships. I try not to have too many, but I have a couple large annual sponsors like Hilton, Chase, and Kroger. We vet each opportunity. I think that's better, too, from

> "
> *I'm a* REGULAR PERSON.
> *I'm from* THE SOUTH.
> I LOVE FOOD.
> *I'm not on some*
> *starvation diet.*
> *It's a* MUCH MORE
> PRACTICAL MESSAGE.

a messaging standpoint, so you don't look like a NASCAR driver and your community doesn't look like a big ad. I also make money through the FitMenCook app, which does amazingly well. It's been in the top three food and drink apps since 2015. I'm also publishing a cookbook.

I'm a regular person. I'm from the South. I love food. I'm not on some starvation diet. It's a much more practical message. I'm also a guy. I think all of this makes me stand out in the healthy cooking space.

One of the most satisfying things about social media is that there is no better feeling than posting a recipe online, and then maybe an hour or two later you've got people sending you messages, showing you their version of the same recipe. The way that people comment and tag each other and say, "Hey, this is our Friday game night recipe." Or they send me pictures and stories of their weight loss. I can see the fruits of my labor, and that's what motivates me even more to stay in this space.

OVERCOME HURDLES, TRIUMPH AT A NEW CHALLENGE, INSPIRE, REPEAT

ALANA NICHOLS

FROM ▸

PROFESSIONAL ADAPTIVE SKIER

TO ▸

PROFESSIONAL ADAPTIVE SURFER

"It wasn't until I accepted my life as it was that doors started opening."

ALANA NICHOLS HAS ALWAYS had the drive to win, defining herself as an athlete and competitor since she was in grade school. By senior year, the star athlete was fielding offers for a softball scholarship.

Then one afternoon of snowboarding changed everything. While attempting her first-ever backflip, Alana fell, landing on a boulder obscured by the snow. She was paralyzed from the waist down upon impact.

Despite spending four months in the hospital, Alana managed to graduate with her class and start at the University of New Mexico. But the life she had, and the life she imagined for herself, no longer existed. She had thrived on her strength, but, confined to a wheelchair, she felt the opposite. "For so long my identity was about being an athlete," she explains. "I was all about setting goals and achieving them. That's where I got my confidence. So when I didn't have those endorphins running through me, I felt depressed and hopeless."

Two years later, Alana happened upon a game of wheelchair basketball in the university's gym. Though they were in wheelchairs, the athletes weren't holding back. The game was intense and the competition fierce. Alana was riveted. "Right after my injury, I more or less fought this experience of being a newly spinal cord–injured person, and that's fair. Of course I don't want to be paralyzed, of course I'm going to fight it. But it wasn't until I accepted my life as it was that doors started opening. I started being open to sports again, and that is when wheelchair basketball came into my life."

> **"**
> *Getting out on the ocean helped me feel strong again. It gave me the space I needed from skiing to heal and to get some perspective.*

Alana tried playing basketball again, and the drive to succeed and the fun of it all came back to her. At times it was frustrating to adapt to

playing in a wheelchair, but the challenge motivated her. She transferred to the University of Arizona to be a part of their program. Alana qualified for the US Women's Wheelchair Basketball National Team in 2005. In 2008, they brought home a gold medal. "Being on the podium and thinking back to where I was when I broke my back," she recalls, "there was just this incredible feeling of accomplishment."

Alana realized that if she could play basketball, she could also tackle other sports. She set her sights on adaptive skiing—and the 2010 Paralympic Winter Games in Vancouver, Canada. With training she made it, and at the Winter Games she took home two gold medals, a silver, and a bronze. In 2011, at the International Paralympic Competition, she won the Alpine Skiing World Championships and was named Paralympic Athlete of the Year. "I'm a thrill seeker, so monoskiing was perfect for me. I loved going fast."

Alana's next goal? The 2014 Paralympics in Sochi. However, while training in Oregon, Alana had a major accident. She skied into a boulder, broke both of her ankles, and dislocated her right shoulder, which had to be reconstructed. "I was in a sling for six weeks and down to one working limb," she says. But she refused to let the accident prevent her from going; she spent a couple of months in rehab and made it to the Games.

At Sochi she started out strong. She won a silver medal in the downhill. Then in the Super G race she fell, knocking herself unconscious, dislocating her jaw, and requiring six stitches. A master at overcoming hurdles, she managed to ski another race just days later, coming in fourth place. However, the Sochi experience made her reevaluate everything. She needed a break from skiing.

Alana tapped into her remarkable ability to pivot, finding another opportunity to ace another sport. While on a vacation with her grandmother in Hawaii, she discovered adaptive surfing—a sport she hadn't known existed. "Surfing found me at just the right time. Getting out on the ocean helped me feel strong again," she says. "It gave me the space I needed from skiing to heal and to get some perspective." Not only that, it gave her a chance to compete again. In 2015, just a year after Sochi, she came in seventh at the Stance ISA World Adaptive Surfing Championship. She was the only woman to compete.

Surfing also gave Alana the confidence to ski competitively again. She was signed up to compete as a skier at the 2018 Winter Paralympics in PyeongChang when she had a fall during a qualifying race. Suffering from a concussion, she had to choose her health over the sport and never made it there. Reluctantly, she retired from professional skiing. "It feels weird," Alana admits. "I am reinventing myself again."

Alana is now focused on public speaking, surfing, and getting more disabled athletes to discover the exhilaration of riding the waves. She was recently named to the International Surf Association Athletes' Commission board. "It's a real honor to be chosen, to have the responsibility to shape the direction we move in, with the ultimate goal of getting adaptive surfing onto a Paralympic platform.

Even more important is to spread adaptive surfing around the world to give people an opportunity to feel that same amazing sense of freedom that I get in the water."

For Alana, the past year has been another one of unexpected detours, and she is still trying to decide exactly what the future will hold for her as an athlete. However, Alana recognizes she's been in that place before countless times and each time, despite the unbelievable hurdles she's faced, she always landed in a place of adventure, challenge, and, ultimately, confidence. She has faith that it will happen again. "I just keep reminding myself to be okay in the unknowingness," she says. "I know my path is developing."

ADAPT TO
CHANGE

*After a snowboarding accident left her paralyzed,
Alana Nichols thought her dreams of being a professional athlete were
over. However, she has gone on to win Paralympic medals in
basketball and skiing, and now she is tackling adaptive surfing.
Alana shares her top five tips for those rebuilding their life or
unexpectedly changing course.*

1

DON'T GO THROUGH IT ALONE

Find a tribe of people who support you and understand what you are going through, and be open to receiving their help. We aren't meant to go through this life alone and certainly not at the toughest of times. Often we isolate and shut down when we are struggling, but nothing could be more counterproductive to growing and moving through a change. It's surprisingly healing and helpful just to talk about how you feel as you transition.

2

EXERCISE

You will feel better immediately, and it works every time. Thirty minutes of any physical movement will help kick-start your momentum when you are going through difficult times.

3

DEVELOP A MANTRA

Try to boil down all your thoughts into one encouraging theme. Keep it simple so that you can easily focus on it. For example, "Can't go back, only forward" or "Clear the path." Breathe deeply, and repeat as often as you need to.

BE GRATEFUL

It is essential to my life to wake up and spend time acknowledging what I am grateful for. Even being thankful for the lesson that hardship is teaching you can change your perspective. Saying "I'm so grateful for this wheelchair" was hard. But once I did, there was this new understanding about how lucky I am to even have a wheelchair.

ACCEPT THINGS AS THEY ARE, EVEN IF YOU DON'T WANT TO

The most important piece for me when dealing with struggle is acknowledging that the transition is equally as important to growth as success is. Simply acknowledging the hardship helps. The sooner you accept what you are going through, the sooner you realize the struggle is not going to last forever and you can, and will, move forward.

7

BECOME A
PROFESSIONAL
FOODIE

*Make Your Hobby Your Career / Start a Winery /
Skip Culinary School and Learn on the Job /
Realize Your Dream / Live off the Land*

YOU HAVE A PENCHANT FOR INTENSE FLAVORS. You don't need a recipe; you see cooking as more of an art, not a paint-by-numbers experience. You're fascinated by the science of cooking, how different combinations of foods can yield such a variety of tastes.

There's also the social aspect. Where are we in our most celebratory moments? Whether sitting around a table or toasting to the future, there is a sort of magic in how a great meal or an incredible bottle of wine brings people together.

When you've mastered the art of food, the question is, can you master the business side? Do you dream of opening your own restaurant? Launching your own line of food products? Are you ready to trade your office for a vineyard? Do you want to raise chickens or grow vegetables? Do you want to try to live off the land? The stories in this chapter showcase several different sides of the culinary landscape: winemakers, chefs, restaurant owners, and farmers. They share the joys and challenges of trying to make it in the food world.

Are you ready to dig in?

MAKE YOUR
HOBBY
YOUR CAREER

JAMIE KUTCH

FROM

—

WALL STREET TRADER

TO

—

WINERY OWNER

I **WAS ALWAYS A HOBBY** guy. As a kid I played every sport imaginable, I tap-danced, I did magic. When I was living in Manhattan and drinking lots of wine, I was learning everything I could. I sneaked into trade tastings, hunting for rare bottles of wine. I logged on to wine chat boards. After college, I succumbed to the desire to make money, so I went to Wall Street, but it is so cutthroat that the boards were my outlet.

I interviewed at Cantor Fitzgerald right before 9/11, and that shook me up enough to start to research getting away from the financial world in Manhattan. I talked to wine shop owners and learned about wine sales positions and distributors. I conjured up the idea that the ultimate career would be to be a winemaker. I started to network on the Robert Parker chat board, commenting on wine I thought was fantastic.

I heard about a small specialty wine by Michael Browne, and I emailed him to see if I could get a bottle. That same day he wrote me back, saying he would send me one from his own stash as all the others were accounted for. I thanked him and mentioned how envious I was that he was living my dream. He said, "My advice is go for your dream, otherwise you might regret it for the rest of your life. If you think this is your calling: drop everything you are doing and sacrifice a few years to get where you want to be. That is what I did, and it is going in a very good direction." At the end of the email, Michael said he would help me make my dream a reality and mentor me in my goal of making wine under my very own label.

My uncle once told me that there are one or two opportunities in your lifetime where you have to take a big risk, and if you do it the rewards will be so great. It makes you think about the outcome for yourself, your future, your happiness, your relationship, your finances. When I heard from Michael, it shook me. What if I actually did this? I talked it through with my parents and my girlfriend. Everyone supported my decision. I was moving to California.

I moved into a tiny one-bedroom apartment and lived out of a suitcase and on an air mattress for six months. The first year I wasn't getting paid, but I had saved enough that I could do it.

As an apprentice under Michael, I was thrown into everything. I started preparing for harvest, tasting berry samples, deciding what to pick, sorting fruit, fermenting, putting it into the barrel. I knew I needed to come out of the experience ready to launch my own wine.

After the year was up, I made a deal with one grower and picked out a few tons of fruit to start making my own wine. I started at 150 cases. I had learned enough about what makes a great wine to be able to decide how to make my own. I am a type A compulsive personality, so I was driven to make the best Pinot Noir out there.

The wine chat room was instant marketing. When I posted that I was going to become a winemaker, before I even left New York, I had four hundred people say they wanted to try my wine. So I had a targeted customer base, all before I started Kutch Wines.

Patience is the biggest challenge. You have to wait a few years before you are ready to sell. Wine is a very patient industry; the longer you do it, the more success you can have. It's the opposite of Wall Street. There at age 30 you actually start to decline compared to people who are younger, newer, faster, more energy driven.

I am living a totally different life than I did in New York. I wake up at 5 or 5:30, and it is still dark out. I drive two hours to the coast and stand in a vineyard that is utterly quiet. I look out and see the Pacific and feel the cool breeze. Looking at the grapes and having the realization that my hands are going to make wine out of that. Working with Mother Nature and hoping that she will work with us—it is so rewarding.

When you get a message that someone celebrated their birthday or anniversary with your wines or customers are so excited about what you are making, you think, *I actually created something, instead of just creating wealth for Merrill Lynch.*

I don't do this job to have a Ferrari in the driveway. If I wanted to do that, I would have stayed on Wall Street. Though we live in a supersize-me nation, I have found a balance and happiness staying small. Right now I have one employee. I would need more employees to make more wine. More doesn't equal better in my eyes. I cut it off at 3,000 cases a year.

In life what is important is to do what you love. I wouldn't sell my brand for any amount of money. I would be perplexed about what it is I would do for happiness after that.

START A
WINERY

Want to move to wine country as Jamie Kutch did? Here are his top five pieces of advice.

1

TRAVEL AND TASTE A LOT OF WINE

Each region has its own mythology, techniques, style, and opinions on winemaking. The more knowledge you have on the variety of methods and what creates a range of tastes, the better your own product will be.

2

TALK TO THE EXPERTS

Once you have chosen region and grape variety, you need to talk to everyone who has worked with those grape varieties. The old guard will have opinions that radically differ from those of the new, younger generation of producers. By speaking with both, you will learn to develop your own opinions, which will help form your own style.

3

SMELLING AND TASTING ARE YOUR TOOLS

Smell anything and everything you can from flowers to berries to grass to even a handful of dirt. Scent will help you choose when to pick your grapes and how much to extract from them and know whether things are working or not during the fermentation and aging process.

4

WORK FOR FREE

Reach out to winemakers and offer to apprentice. Be open to working a harvest for free. It isn't difficult to make wine, but it is difficult to make great wine. Learning from others is a crucial step to becoming great.

5

DON'T HAVE A PLAN B

If you believe you will succeed, you cannot fail. For me, failure wasn't an option, as I was well aware of what it was like working in a cubicle with halogen lights overhead. Now when I look up, I usually see a blue sky, the occasional hawk, and vineyards as far as the eye can see.

LEARN
ON THE
JOB

FROM  **TO**

—

**COMMERCIAL
REAL ESTATE AGENT**

—

**RESTAURANT
OWNER AND CHEF**

T**HE HEAD CHEF TURNED** owner of the Beatrice Inn is earning accolades many in the food world only dream of. When Angie's restaurant was reviewed in the *New York Times* they raved, "By following her gut, she has made the Beatrice Inn one of the most celebratory restaurants in the city." In 2017, she was the only chef from New York to be given the coveted *Food & Wine* Best New Chef award. Just a few years earlier, Angie was living a very different life in commercial real estate. Angie shares her advice for would-be chefs.

CASHING IN I grew up with a very profound love of food. My aunt was Ruby Chow, the Seattle restaurateur. But my family didn't want me to go into the restaurant business, they wanted something different for me. I went to college for a little while but dropped out. I was more interested in making money, so I entered the school of hard knocks. I moved to LA and went into commercial real estate. I worked for Colliers International for years—that's where I got my education.

OPTING OUT I was not fulfilled in the corporate world at all, but I was making a ton of money. By all standards my life was pretty amazing, but it wasn't for me. I ended up leaving my job and not knowing what I wanted to do. I traveled for several months, and so much of my trip was about food. I realized I was happiest when I was cooking.

GOING TO CULINARY SCHOOL I spent the rest of my savings and dumped it into culinary school in New York. It was easy—and it was a complete waste of my time and money. Culinary schools back in the day had a longer program that was two or three years. Now they have courses on how to get a TV show.

LEARNING BY DOING I had a job before I knew anything, and that's where I learned. I worked at Marlow & Sons and Diner, and opened Reynard with Andrew Tarlow. I learned so much working at Diner. It was like the Wild West. We would literally be changing the menu every single day. It was "Take everything out and make something great." That's where I learned how to cook. Then I worked for April Bloomfield at the Spotted Pig. She gave me a commitment to perfection that I didn't know existed. She taught me how to take my time and focus on the details. April taught me how to run a restaurant.

MAKING LESS FOR A WHILE Money is always a big factor. I went from making six figures a year to peeling onions and shucking oysters for $10 an hour. For a lot of people, the financial aspect would be tremendously off-putting. I have gone from making a lot to being broke to making a lot again. Money is money, and you can always make more of it. So not having it is not something I can ever worry about. Doing something I love has made the difference for me.

> "
> *By all standards
> my life was*
> PRETTY
> AMAZING,
> *but it wasn't for me.*

SEIZING OPPORTUNITY WHEN IT KNOCKS When I was at the Spotted Pig, the old owners of the Beatrice Inn found me to see if I would be interested in the chef position there. I said no for about three months. The restaurant had a tumultuous history, and I didn't want to leave my job. But I realized if I didn't go and if I didn't do my own thing, I would be cooking someone else's food for the rest of my life.

GOING FROM CHEF TO OWNER I was a chef at Beatrice for two years, and I bought Graydon Carter out. He has always been such a huge supporter and a mentor, it worked out well. My father always said if you are going to make money, make it with family. My business partner is my cousin, and my brothers have a web design company, so they design my menu and business cards. It is truly just us.

DEVELOPING BUSINESS SAVVY I come from a business world. I am very thankful to have the background that I have. A lot of people in our industry don't understand labor costs, P & L, and accounting. I am just really thankful that I had that experience and I know how to do all those things. Yes, I am a chef and a cook, but you can't be creative if you can't pay the bills.

TEACHING YOUNG CHEFS What's really exciting for me is to teach the next generation of cooks. I don't think that the culinary schools are doing it. I want to fill my kitchen with kids who are tremendously excited to be there. They need to have passion, and we can cultivate the work ethic. A measure of my success is where they are in five years and in ten years. I want these guys running their own kitchens within the next eight to ten years.

MOVE TO
PARADISE
AND TAKE YOUR
JOB WITH YOU

CARRIE & JERRY BOGAR

FROM

RESTAURANT
OWNERS IN
PENNSYLVANIA

TO

RESTAURANT
OWNERS IN
ANGUILLA

FOR OVER A DECADE, we ran a fine dining fifty-seat restaurant in central Pennsylvania. Unexpectedly, we were approached by a developer who was working on a five-hundred-acre parcel and wanted to include a 120-seat restaurant. We drew up plans, and everything looked really good. But one day we looked at each other and thought, *This is going to be a lot more work.* At that point, we had been basically working all year to take one or two weeks off. We spent the first week of January at a different island every year. We thought, *This is kind of stupid. We don't need to work all year to save to go to the Caribbean, we could open a restaurant there and live there.*

We did a Google search for "Caribbean restaurant for sale," and spots in Anguilla and Nevis popped up. We had been to Nevis but thought it might not have the volume of established tourism that we would probably need. We had never been to Anguilla before, but we knew it had a cachet of having a high-end clientele and good restaurants.

We flew down to Anguilla and stayed for five days. We ate in all the top-end restaurants to see what the competition would be. We figured we had the know-how; we had been running restaurants for twelve years. We thought the chances were pretty good we would do all right.

When we met with the owners of the restaurant for sale, they were thankfully more interested in what kind of people we were rather than money. We said, "This is the deal. We have to sell everything back home first. We don't have any money until we do." They are very laid-back buyers and have another business, so they were okay with waiting. They wanted buyers who weren't going to have loud music or a night-club atmosphere. They told us, "A handshake is good enough for us." And we had a deal. We kept flying down every three months to shake their hands and find a house and schools for the kids.

When we flew back to Pennsylvania, we went back, told our staff, and put everything on the market. But it took forever to sell our restaurant. The first year we had a buyer, but she got sick and wasn't able to do it. After the end of the second year, a chain restaurant offered us a huge amount of money for the liquor license. We felt like it was selling our soul a little bit. It enabled us to do what we wanted to do, but it was hard to see our work get dismantled like that.

While our sale was being finalized, we went down to shake the restaurant owners' hands again, and they said, "We've been talking about it, we decided not to sell." We couldn't believe it. But they offered to lease it to us. We bought a house and signed a ten-year lease for Veya.

It is a lot less stressful here. Everyone here is in a laid-back frame of mind. In Pennsylvania, when the purveyors would come for deliveries, they would be running around and hustling. We would have to check to see if they were ripping us off. In Anguilla the fisherman comes in and it's like, "How are your kids? How are you doing? How are the seas?" We have to allow more time to get things done, but it's nice time. It's across the board like that. If we go to the grocery store, it's going to take an hour because we are going to run into twenty people to talk to. We like that.

In Pennsylvania, we would work six days and people would get all weird if we closed for a day. When we got to Anguilla, people were like, "You're really going to work six days a week? Are you nuts? You're going to be tired! Why don't you work five days a week? When it's slow, why don't you work four? Everyone will still come because they are on vacation!" We now serve only one meal a day, because it is a better pace.

Instead of taking off two weeks a year for vacation, we take two months off during hurricane season, October and November. It's not that unusual in the Caribbean, as many people work in hospitality and those are the quietest months. Our children's teachers give us their work for that time, and our children do a report when

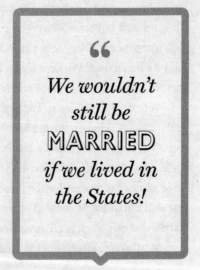

> "
> *We wouldn't
> still be*
> MARRIED
> *if we lived in
> the States!*

they get back. It's a lot more laid-back and understanding. We could not take the kids out of school for two months in the States. We travel everywhere and seek out unusual things to do and eat. We've been to Costa Rica, Scotland, Botswana, and Vietnam.

We wouldn't still be married if we lived in the States! It's so stressful trying to compete and trying to keep up—unemployment compensation, insurance, taxes, and you can't even do what you like to do because you're so buried deep in that. When you are constantly going going going, you don't have time to think. You don't have time to come up with new ideas. You don't even have time to stop. Now it is fewer hours, fewer days, more vacation, and financially better. It was the right move.

REALIZE YOUR
DREAM

FROM
—
HOUSEKEEPER,
BABYSITTER

TO
—
OWNER OF
A MEXICAN FOOD
CAFÉ

WHEN MARIA SERRANO WAS working at dozens of jobs for dozens of clients—as a babysitter, housekeeper, factory worker, and dry cleaner's assistant—she kept her focus on what the result of all her hard work would be: being her own boss one day. "Cleaning houses was good money but really hard work. In my mind, I thought, *I don't want to keep doing this for the rest of my life. I want something different,*" she explains. "So I knew I had to work very hard and save money so one day I could run a business."

At 18, Maria had left her small town in Mexico to move in with her older sister in Queens, New York, and work in a garment factory. But she didn't mesh with city life and missed the slower pace of a small town. Maria and a friend moved to a small apartment in Southampton, a bucolic beach town on Long Island. There they worked at a dry cleaner's making labels and numbers for clothes. Maria worked there for three years before marrying her now ex-husband and moving to nearby Shelter Island.

On the island, Maria found work babysitting and cleaning houses, working especially closely with one family. When the children got older, Maria assumed she would be out of a job, but her boss was opening a deli on the island and wanted to hire her to work there. Maria was initially reluctant, concerned that she had never worked in food service. "My boss just said, 'Don't worry, you will learn.' And it was true, I learned everything right away." It wasn't long before she was handling every aspect of the business from taking orders to making sandwiches, whipping up soups, and working the register. She worked from 6 a.m. to 3 p.m. and cleaned houses and babysat in the afternoons and on weekends.

Maria found herself especially drawn to the creativity of cooking and the bond around food that happens with customers. "I love to cook, and I liked how people would leave the store so happy," she explains. "Everybody liked my food, and that is really what gave me the inspiration to open my own place one day."

Maria kept the idea in the back of her mind. After four years the deli closed, and she reluctantly went back to cleaning houses full-time. When a new health food restaurant opened on the island, she reached out to a friend of the owner to say she would be interested in cooking. She was hired and again she found herself loving the bond with customers and the fun of creating her own items on the menu. But when the business began to flounder, Maria, now divorced with two children, grew concerned that she would lose another job. "I told the owner, 'If one day you want to sell the business, I really want to buy it.'" Maria was smart to speak up. The owner took her up on her offer.

Maria reached out to an attorney to help her through the process of buying the business. She used the money she had saved from cleaning houses, plus a loan from her sister, to start. After the negotiating was finalized, Maria was handed the keys in January, when the island is at its quietest.

Paying rent, legal fees, permits, and insurance meant she couldn't afford to wait for income to come in. Maria opened in April 2012 with a mix of Mexican food, healthy options, and juices. Over time, she saw what sold and refined her menu. Maria's Kitchen is now a combination of café, take-out spot, and health food store.

The first summer was a huge success, and Maria immediately invested in buying new refrigerators and kitchen appliances. She wasn't prepared for business to quiet down drastically in the winter, when the island population goes from around 10,000 to 2,000. "I didn't save any money for the winter," she admits. "Then winter came, and it was very slow. I was thinking, *I am not going to make it!*" The next summer season helped her get back on course, but the following years held challenges. "In three years I didn't see any money for myself." She even moved in with her ex for a little while to save on rent.

After three years, she extended her hours, working twelve-hour days, seven days a week, to move out on her own with the children. Maria's Kitchen has now been open for five years, and she has worked out the kinks. "Now everything is better. My business is doing very well. Every summer is great, winter it's not really that much, but now I have a regular paycheck. I know how to make everything work," she explains. "I am so happy that I made my dreams happen."

LIVE OFF THE
LAND

CHRIS HOLMAN

FROM ▶

**ARABIC
LANGUAGE TEACHER**

TO ▶

FARMER

I **WASN'T PLANNING ON BECOMING** a farmer. I was midcareer working as one of the two or three non-native Arabic teachers in the United States, but I had a nine-month gap to fill before I started my PhD program at the University of Wisconsin. My in-laws raised about fifty chickens a year, and I wanted to try it. My wife, Maria, and I thought we could raise some chickens, save some money, and sell to some friends.

We rented some land from Maria's parents two hours from Madison and started with four hundred chickens. We went with a Redbro variety, a chicken that is much better at foraging in a pasture situation. It was about $500 for the birds, $700 for a shelter, then another $100 for feeders and water. One of the reasons we started with chickens is that they are very resilient, you can set them up with food and water for the week. Maria's mom would go check on them, and we would come up every weekend.

At the time, Maria was working at a restaurant, and when they heard we were raising chickens, they asked to try a few. We had an order for three chickens a week. I thought we were knocking it out of the park! Then another restaurant asked for forty chickens a week, which was $1,700 a year. It was that fork in the road.

> " Becoming a farmer made me focus on WHAT MATTERS.

I was supposed to start my program, but my PhD began to feel like a flaming hula hoop to get a little more money and a little more respect. I really liked farming. I thought I could start the farm, and if it blew up I could always go back to school.

When I told people in the academic world that I was farming, they couldn't understand what I was doing. People in the farming world don't understand why I did it, either. It clearly looks like a step back in many ways. It has been difficult to kind of reconcile the path I was on with a new reality that reflects a different approach to life.

We took most of our life savings, about $30,000, and folded it into starting up Nami Moon Farms. The first year we raised 3,600 chickens. We knew we had a buyer for 1,700 plus a couple hundred for the Tornado Steak House. That put us into marketing mode to figure out how to sell the rest. With pasture-raised chickens we knew we had a niche that would help us stand out.

We have diversified to add more to our business model. We added turkeys, then vegetables, fruit, then eggs. We raise pigs now; we can get a better profit margin on pork, and you don't have a ton of labor. We are reshuffling the operation so we better realize the profit potential of every hour that I work.

There are a lot of perks to farming: good health, a closer connection to my family and my community. There is a real sense of belonging. There is also something about growing and selling food to someone who shares it with their family. I love that process. I also like being a part of a strong community that I am active in and connected to. Becoming a farmer made me focus on what matters.

We have become pretty well known in the state, so I use the platform that we have to remain an educator. I encourage discussion about food and food production and try to get people to think more critically. I present on farming at a variety of conferences, including the Wisconsin Farmers Union's annual convention, the Global Forum for Food and Agriculture, and at the White House, where I represented small-farm perspectives on supply chains, market access, and infrastructure. It is a side of my brain that I didn't want to leave behind. Promoting dialogue really matters to me. That has been and will remain a constant in my life.

BECOME FAMOUS IN A
FOREIGN COUNTRY

JULIE DEFFENSE

FROM

MAGAZINE
PUBLISHER

TO

WEDDING CAKE
DESIGNER

I N COLLEGE, I STUDIED architecture in Italy for a semester. I loved it so much I looked for every chance I could to go back. After graduation, I was offered a three-month paid internship in web design in Portugal through a colleague of my father's. At the time, I was living at home in the suburbs of Philadelphia, working in graphic design for the yellow pages. I was like a robot there. I got paid per ad. I got a bonus for not having any typos. I would go to bed at 8:30 p.m. because I had to get up so early. I had no social life.

Even though I really knew only one person in Portugal and didn't speak a word of Portuguese, I thought the internship would be an awesome adventure. I am so grateful that I went, because I never would have met my husband, Jacques, and I never would've found what I was meant to do in life.

As excited as I was to go, I cried every single day for the first month. All my friends were following mega–career paths in NYC or Boston. They were jealous of me and the decision that I made to move to Europe, and I was jealous of them and worried I had made a huge mistake. I was in Portugal without any friends and not knowing the language. I remember calling my parents so many times that they finally said, "These calls are costing a fortune, you need to toughen up and make some friends."

A few weeks later, I met Jacques. We hit it off, and basically that was it, we were inseparable. Toward the end of my internship, my company took a downward turn and ended up closing. I decided to take a chance and stay in Portugal, find another job, and see what happened with Jacques.

I sent out more than three hundred CVs and ended up getting a bunch of graphic design freelance work. One of the jobs was working at a magazine as an art director. When my boss retired several years later, I bought it and ran it for a few years, then sold it to start my own magazine.

When I was little, I used to tell my mom that I wanted to be part of a big family, and she always replied, "Be careful what you wish for." Jacques is one of eleven siblings. There are about thirty-five nieces and nephews, so there is always a party, and I began baking cakes for everyone's parties, which I absolutely loved.

I liked baking so much that I took the Wilton School of Cake Decorating and Confectionery Art's master course in the United States, half for fun, half with hopeful intentions. I put an ad in my magazine to try to drum up interest for a new wedding cake side business. Within one month, I had more requests for cakes than advertising revenue for the magazine. I looked at Jacques, and we simultaneously decided that

I should make a career change, quick. I closed the magazine, freeing me to do what I really wanted to.

I am so glad that I took the risk. My business has been really successful. I have worked hard to become the leading cake designer in Portugal. I focus mainly on weddings and big events. I've also had the opportunity to write and publish three cookbooks here. People stop me in the streets for an autograph, which I find very charming.

There were many times I wished I had stayed in the United States and followed a conventional path and earned lots of money, but deep down I know I wouldn't have been as happy. I grew so much from all the challenges that came with adapting to a different culture. Learning a new language took me a long time. I was embarrassed to make a mistake, so I never said a word in public for a good ten years. Then I did a morning TV segment promoting my first book and spoke for twenty-five minutes in Portuguese. All of our friends were so shocked. I actually learned from watching television and listening to my husband.

When you live abroad, you feel like a lot of your friends back home kind of disappear because everyone has their own lives. Yet you don't really fit into the culture where you do live. Then you go back home and you think, *I don't really fit in here, either.*

One of my goals was to be able to have businesses both in Portugal and in the States, to be closer to my family and friends. I started by making wedding cakes in the Boston area on request, and I have now established a business in Sarasota, Florida, where I will be for six months a year. I had to start from zero and build up a business here while at the same time maintaining everything in Portugal.

When I first moved to Portugal, I was told by a friend that women didn't really have careers here, so I shouldn't expect to have the same type of career path and growth that I would have had if I stayed in the States. Looking back at what I've accomplished, I am happy to say I am pretty sure I proved otherwise.

ACKNOWLEDGMENTS

---

*I first had the idea for this book
more than a decade ago.*

I HAD A DIFFERENT AGENT THEN. I wasn't as confident. It didn't make it past the initial pitch. But after writing seven books as a ghostwriter, I was ready to see my name back on a book cover. I met an incredible agent, Alison Fargis, who agreed. She helped me publish another idea I had for years (*Hotel Chic at Home*! Buy it!). Next we revamped the concept for *Take the Leap*. I'm so grateful for her cheerleading, guidance, and adept agenting. Plus she paired me with the best editor I have ever had over the course of eleven books. Cara Bedick got the idea right away and has been such a great partner at every step. I'm so proud of the work we've done together.

A million thanks to the sixty-plus people who let me ask them very personal questions and pepper them with way too many follow-up emails. I'm so inspired by every one of their powerful stories and so happy they let me share them.

Thank you to Laura Palese for her spot-on cheery book design, Lara Blackman and Rebecca Strobel for all of their help.

A special thank you and unending gratitude to Alexandra Perron, Anne Kvinge, and Lila Claghorn, without whom this book might have taken another year.

And of course a million hugs to my hubby, kiddos, and entire family.

PHOTO CREDITS

PAGE 18: Photo of Lauryn Kahn, credit Aleksandar Letic

PAGE 23: Photo of Lisa Congdon, credit Kimberley Hasselbrink, 2016

PAGES 28, 30: Photo of Amy Chu, credit Adrian Chang

PAGE 34: Photo of Tess Finnegan, credit Kate Noelle Photography

PAGE 37: Photo of Suysel dePedro Cunningham, credit Trevor Tondro

PAGE 41: Photo of Danielle Mastrion, credit to artist Danielle Mastrion

PAGE 42: Photo of Danielle Mastrion in front of mural created in collaboration with Danielle Mastrion, Tommy Holiday, Sam Moses for Denos Wonder Wheel Park, credit Miranda Maxwell

PAGE 45: Photo of Simon Doonan, credit Albert Sanchez

PAGE 47: Photo of Simon Doonan, credit Michael Childers

PAGES 49, 50, 53: Photo of Jill Kargman, credit Pamela Berkovic

PAGES 56, 58: Photo of Leonard Kim, credit Joshua M. Shelton (headshot), credit Evan Duning (sitting)

PAGES 61, 62: Photo of Katie Warner Johnson, credit Carbon 38

PAGE 64: Photo of Tiffany Pham, credit Audrey Froggatt

PAGE 67: Photo of Jeffrey Nash, credit Poon Watchara-Amphaiwan

PAGE 70: Photo of Patricia Cusden, credit Simon Songhurst

PAGE 74: Photo of Jon Deng, credit Jon Deng

PAGE 78: Photo of Ge Wang, credit Billy Rood

PAGE 83: Photo of Barbara Corcoran, courtesy of Leslie Rodriguez

PAGE 84: Photo of Monique Greenwood, credit OWN: Oprah Winfrey Network

PAGE 90: Photo of Bobbi Brown, credit Morgane Lay

PAGE 94: Photo of Brittany and Scott Meyers, credit Brittany and Scott Meyers

PAGE 99: Photo of Brittany Meyers, credit Brittany and Scott Meyers

PAGE 100: Photo of Ashley Blaylock, credit Jerson Barboza

PAGES 104, 106, 107: Photo of Allison Fleece and Danielle Thornton, credit Ren Fuller

PAGE 108: Photo of Marina De Lima, credit Tomas Woodhall Ochoa

PAGE 112: Photo of Nadia Aly, credit Nadia Aly

PAGE 116: Photo of Talley Smith, credit James Tyrrell

PAGES 120, 122, 123: Photo of Eulanda Shead Osagiede and Omo Osagiede, credit Eulanda Shead Osagiede, credit Cassandra Wilson

PAGES 126–129: Photos of Oneika Raymond, credit Oneika Raymond

PAGES 132, 133: Photo of Scott Neeson, credit Scott Rotzoll

PAGE 137: Photo of Terri Cole, credit Kinothèque

PAGE 141: Photo of Adam Braun, credit GenMotion

PAGES 142, 145: Photo of Aaron Maybin, credit Kyle Pompey

PAGES 146, 147: Photo of Nicole Laterra, credit Nicole LaTerra

PAGE 150, 153: Photo of Bren Smith, credit Ron Gautreau

PAGE 154: Photo of Carlye Hughes, credit Roy O'Dell

PAGES 157, 159: Photo of Aaron Walker, credit Camelback Ventures

PAGE 164: Photo of Noëlle Santos, credit Cynthia Ciccone

PAGE 168: Photo of Angie Banicki, credit Sami Drasin

PAGE 172: Photo of Marjorie Gubelmann, credit BFA for Dolce & Gabbana

PAGE 175: Photo of Steve Gorman, credit Kaitlyn Huerta

PAGE 181: Photo of Jason Carden, credit MirMir Photo Booth @ mirmir.com

PAGE 184: Photo of Carolyn Waters, credit Mia D'Avanza

PAGE 190: Photo of Eric Gorges, credit Roe Photo

PAGE 193: Photo of Nancy Cooley, credit Axel Dupeux / Redux

PAGE 198: Photo of Robert Hammond, credit Liz Ligon, courtesy of Friends of the High Line

PAGE 204: Photo of Maggie Guterl, credit Myke Hermsmeyer/Trail Racing Over Texas

PAGE 207: Phot of Stacy Bare, credit Tappan Brown

PAGE 211: Photo of Judson Kauffman, credit Korey Howell

PAGES 212, 214: Photo of Payal Kadakia, credit Neelam Shah (dancing), credit Ros Hayes (headshot)

PAGE 215: Photo of Agatha Achindu, credit Cynthia Hauser at Five Arrows Photography

PAGE 219: Photo of Jennifer Gefsky, credit Carolyn Simpson, Doublevision Photographers

PAGE 220: Photo of Kevin Curry, credit Kevin Curry

PAGES 223, 225: Photo of Alana Nichols, credit Sydney Prather

PAGE 232: Photo of Jamie Kutch, credit Kutch Wines

PAGE 236: Photo of Angie Mar, credit Eric Vitale

PAGE 240: Photo of Jerry and Carrie Bogar, credit Tamika Lewis

PAGE 244: Photo of Maria Serrano, credit Sara Bliss

PAGE 247: Photo of Chris Holman, credit Chris Holman

PAGE 250: Photo of Julie Deffense, credit Hugo Moura and Bruno Oliveira from Clickt Photography

ABOUT THE AUTHOR

SARA BLISS is a brand advisor, freelance writer, and *New York Times* best-selling author who covers career, business, health, beauty, and travel. Sara is coauthor and author of eleven books, including *Beauty from the Inside Out* and *Hotel Chic at Home*. She is a *Forbes* contributor writing about career pivots. Sara's articles have appeared in the *Wall Street Journal*, *Travel + Leisure*, *Forbes*, and *Money*.